Nicholas P. Wiseman, Samuel H. Turner

Essay on Our Lord's Discourse at Capernaum

recorded in the sixth chapter of St. John, with strictures on Cardinal Wiseman's lectures on the real presence, and notices of some of his errors, both of fact and reasoning

Nicholas P. Wiseman, Samuel H. Turner

Essay on Our Lord's Discourse at Capernaum
recorded in the sixth chapter of St. John, with strictures on Cardinal Wiseman's lectures on the real presence, and notices of some of his errors, both of fact and reasoning

ISBN/EAN: 9783337273040

Printed in Europe, USA, Canada, Australia, Japan

Cover: Foto ©Lupo / pixelio.de

More available books at **www.hansebooks.com**

ESSAY

ON OUR LORD'S

DISCOURSE AT CAPERNAUM,

RECORDED IN THE SIXTH CHAPTER OF ST. JOHN.

WITH

STRICTURES ON CARDINAL WISEMAN'S LECTURES ON THE REAL PRESENCE, AND NOTICES OF SOME OF HIS ERRORS, BOTH OF FACT AND REASONING.

BY SAMUEL H. TURNER, D.D.,

PROFESSOR OF BIBLICAL LEARNING AND INTERPRETATION OF SCRIPTURE IN THE GENERAL THEOLOGICAL SEMINARY OF THE PROTESTANT EPISCOPAL CHURCH; AND OF THE HEBREW LANGUAGE AND LITERATURE IN COLUMBIA COLLEGE, NEW YORK.

Third Edition.

NEW-YORK:
ANSON D. F. RANDOLPH, 683 BROADWAY.
1860.

THE REV. BIRD WILSON, D.D.,

PROFESSOR OF SYSTEMATIC DIVINITY IN THE GENERAL THEOLOGICAL
SEMINARY OF THE PROTESTANT EPISCOPAL CHURCH;

THE BENEFIT OF WHOSE EXTENSIVE LEARNING AND SOUND
JUDGMENT, CONSTANTLY SHOWN IN HIS VALUABLE INSTRUC-
TIONS, THE INSTITUTION HAS LONG ENJOYED; AND
WHOSE UNIFORM KINDNESS AND FRIENDSHIP WILL
ALWAYS BE GRATEFULLY REMEMBERED BY
THE WRITER;

THIS ESSAY,

IN THE HOPE THAT THE GENERAL VIEW TAKEN OF THE SUBJECT
WILL MEET WITH HIS APPROVAL,

IS MOST RESPECTFULLY INSCRIBED,

BY

HIS AFFECTIONATE FRIEND AND BROTHER,

THE AUTHOR.

PREFACE.

As the publication of an Essay on our Lord's discourse recorded in the sixth chapter of St. John may seem to be unnecessary, I think proper to state to the reader some of the reasons which led me to prepare the following treatise.

In lecturing on this Gospel to the theological students under my care, my attention was directed, more than a year ago, by one of them to the Lectures on the Real Presence by NICHOLAS WISEMAN, D.D., the first four professing to prove that doctrine, as it is maintained by the Church of Rome, by an appeal to this chapter. These Lectures, as the preface informs us, were "several times delivered in the English College at Rome, as a portion of the theological course" of instruction there given. On returning to England, the author was induced to publish them, with the intention of doing "ample justice to the line of argument which he had pursued in" certain other lectures, and in order "more fully to develop and justify by proofs the Catholic arguments for the Real Presence." Their repeated delivery at

Rome, and their publication in England, with such views and expectations, sanctioned the presumption that the greatest care had been taken to secure soundness in reasoning and minute correctness in statements. What farther tended to confirm in me this supposition, was information communicated by the same individual, that Dr. Wiseman's book had made a strong impression on the minds of a few most estimable persons well known to him. I was thus led to read the work in question, and its perusal determined me to write the following pages, which will put the reader in possession of some reasons for the opinion which I was compelled to form of the book. I was surprised that any intelligent scholar of respectable acquirements in theology should attach much importance to it as a work of reasoning, and also that a person so distinguished by his own Church should have made such palpably erroneous statements as the Lectures furnish. I have pointed out some which had escaped the notice of Dr. TURTON,* one of the author's English opponents. I

* His book bears the following title: The Roman Catholic Doctrine of the Eucharist considered, in reply to Dr. Wiseman's Argument from Scripture. By THOMAS TURTON, D.D., Regius Professor of Divinity in the University of Cambridge, and Dean of Peterborough, Cambridge, 1837, 8vo. To this work and some smaller treatises, Dr. Wiseman published a reply, dated London, 1839, 8vo.

had no knowledge of this gentleman's publication in reply to the Lectures until I had nearly completed my Essay; and a subsequent examination of it, and also of Dr. Wiseman's answer, and of a still later production by the venerable FABER,* suggested no sufficient reason to induce me to alter the plan of my treatise, or to modify my views either of the Lectures themselves, or of the discourse of our Lord which they profess to explain.

An examination of the four Lectures on this discourse very naturally strengthened an inclination which I had for a considerable time entertained, of writing an exposition of the discourse itself. To exhibit what I conceive to be its true sense and object, is the main design of the Essay, which is intended to be exegetical; and in controverting some views of Dr. Wiseman, my design is chiefly to prepare the way for a proper development of our Lord's meaning. The result is now presented to the reader in this little volume, with the earnest wish and prayer, that a feeble effort to advance the glory of God by an attempt to show the true meaning of a part of his most Holy Word may be accompanied by his blessing.

* Christ's Discourse at Capernaum fatal to the Doctrine of Transubstantiation, &c. By GEORGE STANLEY FABER, B.D., Master of Sherburn Hospital, and Prebendary of Salisbury, 8vo. London, 1840.

The errors of Dr. Wiseman, referred to in the title of this edition, are noted in pages 11, 12, 25–27, 41, 42, 67, 68, 88–91. It is amazing that he should have committed blunders and made statements alike irreconcilable with that ordinary attention which every writer is expected to pay to his subject, and that honesty of purpose which marks the candid man. He misrepresents Tholuck. This may be unintentional. Respecting the use of the word Devil in the Syriac New Testament, he makes a false statement, which a little attention would have enabled him to avoid. He represents a publication of Tittmann with a two-fold title, as if it were two distinct works, when he must have known better, as he actually quotes from the same book. He confounds two different facts in our Lord's life, and this in a course of Lectures repeatedly delivered, thus showing a most extraordinary inattention. He makes an unfounded assertion respecting the time of the institution of baptism, without even an attempt to sustain it by any evidence. And, what is passing strange, he seems to identify the gloss of a late Jewish commentator with the original, which is hundreds of years older. Most, if not all of these errors, are passed over without notice by the English authors who have replied to his book. The position which, as a cardinal in England, Dr. Wiseman now occupies, makes it more proper than ever to guard his readers against implicitly trusting a writer who has thus laid himself open to animadversion.

CONTENTS.

PART I.
Examination of Dr. Wiseman's View . . . . . . Page 1

PART II.
Analysis and Exposition of the Discourse 48

PART III.
View of the Early Fathers, and of some Modern Divines . . 103

ESSAY.

PART I.
EXAMINATION OF DR. WISEMAN'S VIEW.

In order to ascertain the import and true meaning of our Lord's discourse to the Jews recorded in the sixth chapter of St. John's Gospel, it becomes exceedingly important to keep in mind the particular circumstances that gave occasion to it.

On the eastern side of the Sea of Tiberias Jesus had fed an immense multitude, amounting probably to 8000 people,* on five barley loaves and two small fishes, and the fragments that remained after the whole were satisfied were sufficient to fill twelve baskets. This was certainly one of the most extraordinary miracles that he had ever performed, and we are not surprised that the witnesses and subjects of it acknowledge him to be the expected prophet. The erroneousness of their views, however, and the worldly character of their minds, are evident from their intention to seize him and make him king. In order to avoid

---

* Mark, vi., 44, Luke, ix., 14, and John, vi., 14, speak of "about 5000 *men*;" Matthew, xiv., 21, does the same, adding, "besides women and children." John, vi., 2, makes it probable that many of them were sick.

A

the excitement and evils which must have followed such a course, our Lord, after dismissing the crowd, retires, agreeably to his manner, to pray in solitude. At evening his disciples embark in their vessel, with the intention, probably, of stopping farther up on the eastern side of the lake, where their Master would meet them, and then proceeding across to Capernaum, which was situated on the western shore.* But an unexpected storm of wind preventing them from landing, and driving the vessel far into the lake, Jesus appeared to them not long before daybreak† walking on the water. Being received into the vessel, the sea became calm, and they soon reached the destined haven, vi., 1–21.

On the following day, the excited multitude, not finding Jesus, and knowing that he had not embarked with his disciples, and having seen no other vessel than the one occupied by them, procured other vessels and crossed the lake.‡ Finding him at Capernaum, they expressed their wonder at his getting there, 22–25 ; and this is followed by the discourse now to be considered.

In order to ascertain its true meaning, it is important to determine whether the leading subject is throughout the same, or whether a transition must be allowed from one topic to another. Prot-

---

* See Newcome's Harmony, note, § 64.

† Matt., xiv., 24, 25.

‡ It is not necessary to suppose that the whole multitude went over. The Scripture often ascribes to a mass what is strictly applicable to a part only.

estant commentators generally adopt the former view. Among the defenders of the latter Dr. Wiseman stands prominent, and as his book on the Eucharist professedly vindicates this view, and the Romanist doctrine of the Real Presence as supposed to be founded on this chapter, I shall examine the principal arguments alleged by him in confirmation of his theories, as preparatory to any direct analysis of the discourse itself.

The author begins by laying down certain principles of interpretation, the correctness of which is unquestionable, while, at the same time, they recognise the fundamental importance of philological investigation in order to attain a right knowledge of Scripture. In examining our Lord's discourse in this chapter, he admits that, until "the 48th or 51st verse, it refers entirely to believing in him," and that on this point "Protestants and Catholics are equally agreed." But he contends that here "a perfect transition is made from believing in Christ to a real eating of his body and drinking of his blood in the sacrament of the Eucharist," while "the generality of Protestants maintain that no such transition takes place." He argues that "there is a change of subject at the 48th verse," and that "the transition is to a real eating of the body of Christ," p. 50, 51.

Dr. Wiseman considers the 48th and three following verses as " a complete section of itself, verse 47 seeming" to him " to form an appropriate close to a division of discourse, by the emphatic asseveration *amen*" (verily) " prefixed to a manifest summary and epilogue of all the preceding doctrine." If what follows in his first paragraph is intended as proof of this, I am wholly unable to see its bearing, and must therefore pass it over. Not to deprive the more discerning reader, however, of the advantage of the argument, I give it entire, in the author's own words. "'Amen, amen, I say unto you, he that believeth in me hath everlasting life.' Compare verses 35, 37, 45. Verse 48 lays down a clear proposition, 'I am the bread of life,' suggested by the preceding words, and just suited for the opening of a new discourse," p. 52.

His next proof is stated as follows: "But these words are exactly the same as open the first part of our Saviour's lecture at verse 35." Now the sacred "lecture" does not open at verse 35, but with the solemn censure of verse 26: "Verily, verily, I say unto you, ye seek me, not because ye saw the miracles, but because ye did eat of the loaves and were filled." The 34th, "Lord, evermore give us this bread," is merely the expression of desire with which some of his hearers interrupted his discourse, as the woman of Samaria did in John, iv., 15. The author's next remark, that it is "an ordinary form of transition with our Lord, when he applies the same images to different purposes, to repeat the very words by which he originally commenced his discourse," even allowing it to be true, is therefore wholly irrelevant. But, admitting its applicability, the instances he proceeds to give in order to illustrate the fact are not to the point, and his remarks on them neither founded on the evident intention of the divine speaker, nor, in my view, deserving of serious refutation. But that I may not be thought to do injustice to the writer, I quote the whole of his illustrations. " I will give two or three instances," that is, of the "ordinary form of transition" employed by Christ. "In John, x., 11, he says, 'I am the good shepherd;' and he then expatiates upon this character *as it regards himself*, contrasting himself with the hireling, and expressing himself ready to die for his sheep. At verse 14 he repeats the words once more, 'I am the good shepherd,' and explains them *with reference to the sheep*, how they hear and obey him, and how his flock will be increased. Again, John, xv., 1, he commences his discourse by 'I am the true vine,' and applies the figure *negatively* to the consequences of *not* being united to him. Then, at verse 5, he repeats the same words, and explains them *positively* of the fruits produced by those who *do* abide in him.* Exactly in the same manner,

* " I consider the latter clause of verse 15 of the first passage, and verse 6, with the last member of verse 5, in the second, as merely incidental and parenthetic; as I think it will be allowed that the division which I have suggested of each parable is manifest and natural. In this remark I have joined the last member of verse 5 (John, xv.) with verse 6, because it has long struck me that the common division of the verses there is not correct. The reasoning seems hardly conclusive, 'he that abideth in me ... beareth *mu h* fruit, be-in our passage, our Saviour, having spoken of himself as bread, 'I am the living bread,' and expatiated on this thought in respect to his being the spiritual nourishment of the soul by faith, makes the same form of transition to treat of himself as *bread* in another sense, inasmuch as his flesh is our real sustenance."

His " principal motive" for maintaining a transition immediately after verse 47, and the introduction of a new topic at verse 53, is " the parallelism of the members" of the intermediate verses. " Nothing to me can be more striking than the regular arrangement of this discourse from verse 48 to verse 52 inclusively; and whoever understands the principle, and is accustomed to its application, will immediately, upon inspecting the passage, as I have transcribed it, in the original and the version, acknowledge that it stands wholly detached from what precedes down to verse 47, and that no transition can be allowed at any point but that. The following is the whole section of our Saviour's discourse, versicularly arranged:

(*a*) ' I am the bread of life.

(*b*) Your fathers did eat manna (*bread from heaven*, see verses 31, 32) in the desert,

cause without me ye can do *nothing*' (verse 5). But if we put the stop after ' much fruit,' and join what follows to the next verse, we have a most expressive argument. ' Because without me ye can do nothing, if any one remain not in me, he shall be cast forth as a worthless branch,' &c. Of course I need not remind my readers that we owe our present division into verses to the elder Stephanus, who made it for his relaxation *inter equitandum*."—The author's might be thought to have been made *inter dormiendum*.

  (*c*) And are dead.
 (*a*) This is the bread
  (*b*) Descending from heaven, (such),
   (*c*) That if any one eat of it, he may not die.
 (*a*) I am the living bread
  (*b*) Which came down from heaven.
   (*c*) If any man eat of this bread, he shall live forever.

'And the bread which I will give is my flesh for the life of the world.'

" You cannot avoid remarking the nice balance of these lines. All those marked (*a*) contain the same ideas of *bread*, and generally of *life;* the second ones (*b*) speak of the descent of this bread from heaven, contrasted with the manna; the third (*c*) impress its worth in the same comparative view. The last clause sums up and imbodies the substance of the preceding. That repetition of the same idea and phrase, which at first sight appears superfluous in this passage, entirely vanishes upon viewing this arrangement, and there is a beautiful progression of sentiment, which gives a value to every repetition. Not to detain you with too many remarks, I will only instance the progressive character of the lines marked (*c*). The first speaks of the want of an immortalizing quality in manna; the second attributes such a quality to the manna of the new Covenant, but in negative terms, 'that if any one eat of it, he *may not die;*' the third expresses the same sentiment in a positive and energetic form. ' If any man eat of this bread, he *shall live forever.*'" I leave it to Dr. Wiseman and the admirers of his Magnus Apollo in this department of Sacred Literature, Bishop Jebb,* to "remark the nice balance of the lines" in this portion " of our Saviour's discourse, versicularly arranged." I content myself with the remark, that the verses whose members this hermeneutical Procrustes has subjected to his operation, imbody the simple expression of a deeply important truth, rising, as is most natural, and in accordance with our Lord's manner and that of his Evangelist, from a negative intimation to a strong, positive, life-inspiring declaration. Such extravagant abuse of the true principle of Hebrew parallelism tends to degrade this beautiful and poetic characteristic of that sacred and venerable tongue. The limit that separates the sublime from the ridiculous is only one short step.

Dr. Wiseman considers his "attempt to prove that there is a marked division of the discourse" as successful and important. On the former point, the reader must judge. The "importance" of it consists in its removing the "objection, that it is doing a violence to our Saviour's discourse to suppose that he passes from one subject to another where there is nothing to indicate such a transition." "To remove it still farther," he refers to

---

* No disrespect is intended to Bishop Jebb by this remark. Still I cannot but think that he has carried his application of the principles of parallelism to a degree wholly unwarranted, and, indeed, exextravagant. See his Sacred Literature, London, 831, 8vo.

what he is pleased to call "a perfectly parallel instance," in "the 24th and 25th chapters of St. Matthew." "The first part of the discourse contained in these chapters refers entirely to the destruction of Jerusalem. It is acknowledged that its concluding portion is referable only to the final judgment; now where does the transition between the two occur? Why, some of the best commentators, as Kuinoel, and after him Bloomfield, place it at the forty-third verse of the twenty-fourth chapter. Now, if you read that passage attentively, you will be struck with the similarity of this transition to the one I have laid down for the sixth chapter of St. John. In the preceding verse (42) our Lord sums up the substance of the foregoing instruction, just as he does in John, vi., 47. 'Watch ye, therefore, because ye know not at what hour your Lord will come.' 'Amen, amen, I say unto you, he that believeth in me hath everlasting life.' He then resumes apparently the same figure, drawn from the necessity of watching a house, as he does that of bread in our case; but then the conclusion of the discourse points out that the 'coming of the Son of man' now mentioned (verse 44) is no longer the moral and invisible one spoken of in the preceding section (verses 30, 37), but a real and substantial advent in the body (xxv., 31)."

In reference to this intended illustration of the author, I would make two observations: first, the transition spoken of may indeed be found in the

43d verse, but it may also be found with at least as much probability, and in harmony with sound exegetical principles, in the 36th. With the words "that *day* and *hour*," compare verse 42, "ye know not what *hour* your Lord doth come;" verse 44, "in such an *hour* as ye think not, the Son of man cometh;" verse 50, "the Lord of that servant will come in a *day* when he looketh not for him, and in an *hour* that he is not aware of;" xxv., 13, "ye know neither the *day* nor the *hour*." The author's argument assumes the transition to be at the 43d verse; and if this assumption should be unfounded, the "perfect parallel" is no parallel at all. Secondly, there is this striking difference between the discourse in St. Matthew and that in St. John. In the latter no change of subject is either required by the series of instruction, or natural in itself; in the former it is universally granted by judicious expositors that a transition is absolutely necessary, in order to give a fair and intelligible meaning to the language. The latter part of the xxvth chapter contains undeniably a different subject from that which is apparent on the face of the former part of the xxivth.

The author concludes his discussion of this topic by stating, "that a learned and acute modern Protestant commentator has observed, that it is manifest that our Saviour cannot have been understood to continue the same subject at verse 51." It would be unjust to Dr. Tholuck, the expositor referred to, to allow him to be understood as expressing the view which this statement naturally implies. He is explaining the whole portion from verse 51 to verse 59 inclusive, and on citing the latter half of verse 51, "and the bread which I will give is my flesh, which I will give for the life of the world," he remarks, that the language καὶ— δὲ, denoting "a *more extended development* of the thought, shows that Christ does not here express the same that he had declared before." Even these two lines, the latter of which is quoted by the lecturer, might have shown him that Tholuck means to represent our Lord as more fully developing the view already given by adding a particular circumstance of importance. But what estimate must we form of the accuracy of Dr. Wiseman's statements, when we find his author proceeding as follows, *immediately after* the words quoted: "Having represented, *in general*, his appearance in humanity as a divine food, he now intends to show in what respect it is so *particularly*. If his intention had been to express by these words *only the very same* idea before conveyed, no reason can be given why he should change the quite clear expression, 'I am the living bread,' for the somewhat obscure one, 'I will give you my flesh.' The future *I will* give refers to something yet to take place." He means Christ's death, as he afterward explains it. The same judicious distinction between the general thought and a more particular development of it had been clearly stated on the preceding page, where the profoundly learned and pious author remarks that " an accurate examination of the whole connexion, and of the particular phrases employed, shows that a *more special* meaning must be connected with these expressions, namely, that Christ, having before *only in a general way* represented his incarnation as a divine living power, now *makes prominent* what was able, in *a sense altogether peculiar*, to convey that power of life, that is to say, his *redeeming death*, as the crowning point of his redeeming life."* Had Dr. Wiseman read the work to which he refers, in confirmation of his own imagined " transition to a new section of our Lord's discourse ?" and if so, does he call his representation of the author's views a fair one ?†

Dr. Wiseman proceeds, in his second lecture, to adduce farther evidence " that a complete change of topic takes place after the 48th verse." After showing that " the phrases which occur in the first part of the discourse were calculated to convey to the minds of those who heard our Saviour

---

* Commentar zum Evangelio Johannis, Hamburg, 1833, p. 129, 130.

† Wiseman elsewhere does manifest injustice to "this learned and amiable professor," whom he regards " with great personal esteem and friendship," p. 141, 142. Correction in this case, however, can hardly be considered as necessary, as one who knows anything of the character of Tholuck as a commentator will not suspect him of the weakness of rejecting an interpretation, "*because otherwise we must become Catholics!*" He does indeed say, that " if the expressions are not tropical, they would prove too much, namely, the Catholic doctrine." But he does not allege the fact of its being Catholic doctrine as proof of its being too much. He presumes this to be already evident on other grounds.

the idea of listening to his doctrines and believing in him, and the more so, as he positively explained them in that sense," he affirms, " that after the transition a totally different phraseology occurs, which, *to his hearers, could not possibly convey that meaning, nor any other save that of a real eating of his flesh and drinking of his blood,*" p. 59, 60. My purpose confines me to an examination of this last statement.*

After giving several of the clauses which speak of "eating the flesh and drinking the blood," the author proceeds with his comment. This I shall now quote, accompanied by such remarks as appear suited to its character.

" 1. We have seen above, that after our Saviour, in consequence of difficulties found by the Jews, had commenced, at verse 35, to explain his sentiments literally, he never returns again to the figurative expression until after he closes that section at verse 47. If we suppose him to continue the same topic after this verse, we must believe him, after having spent thirteen verses in doing

---

* In illustrating the phraseology of the former portion of the discourse, the author calls our attention to what he considers as "very remarkable," namely, "that never once through this part does our Saviour suffer the idea of *eating him* to escape his lips," p. 63. It is true, he does not employ the language, but let any one compare verses 32, 33, 35, 48, 50, with 57, 58, and he will see that they contain the idea, for they both imply and assert that the bread is to be eaten, and that he is the bread ; verses 51-58 inclusive show plainly that to eat him, which is identical with eating the bread that came down from heaven, and to eat his flesh and drink his blood, are equivalent in meaning.

away with the obscurity of his parabolic expressions, and in giving the explanation of its figures, to return again to his obscure phrases, and to take up once more the use of the same parable, which he had so long abandoned for its literal explanation." To remove the impression intended to be produced by this loose and inaccurate representation, it will be sufficient to remark, that several of the assertions here made are wholly unfounded. So far from the 35th verse beginning a "literal explanation of sentiments" before conveyed by "figurative expression," the very first statement is figurative: "I am the bread of life," and so also is the second: "he that cometh to me shall never hunger." The author must have presumed that the greater proportion of his audience would not read the discourse on which he comments. The docile listener, who has been so trained as to abandon his natural right of inquiring and judging for himself, and who, therefore, acquiesces without examination in the correctness of the statements made in his hearing, imagines that the lecturer's minute and careful investigation must be sufficient warrant for the exposition; whereas, the intelligent reader, who, with independence of mind and careful attention, looks at the discourse for himself, must immediately see that the representation made rests on no solid ground. It is true that, in general, the language of our Lord in several of the verses following the 35th is literal, but this is also true of that which precedes. There is nothing in the whole portion more literal, indeed nothing can possibly be more literal, than his answer to the question, "What shall we do that we may work the works of God? This is the work of God, that ye believe on him whom he hath sent." A similarity pervades the whole portion, and there is no evidence to support such a different mode of representation as is assumed. Of the thirteen verses said to be "spent in doing away the obscurity of parabolic expressions, and in giving the explanation of the figures," three are nothing but a statement of the dissatisfaction of the Jews, and the Saviour's direction to them to cease their murmurings.

"2. We have seen likewise how carefully our Lord avoids, throughout the first part, the harsh expression to *eat him*, even where the turn of his phrase seemed to invite him to use it; on the contrary, in the latter section, he employs it without scruple, and even repeats it again and again. This is a remarkable difference of phraseology between the two sections." The reader may form no very incorrect opinion of Dr. Wiseman's accuracy from this statement. "The harsh expression," which he says is "employed without scruple, and even repeated again and again," occurs once, and only once, in verse 57. The apparently harsher expression, "to eat his flesh and drink his blood," does indeed occur several times in verses 53–56; but this is accounted for by the close connexion in which these verses stand with the preceding one, which informs us that "the Jews strove among themselves, saying, how can this man give us his flesh to eat?" a question which was suggested by our Lord's words recorded immediately before: "the bread that I will give is my flesh, which I will give for the life of the world." Be it noted, also, that this harsher expression occurs nowhere else in the whole discourse; a fact quite consistent with the opinion, that while the phraseology is altered, the idea intended to be conveyed remains the same throughout. No argument can be founded on "our Lord's avoiding," in the early part of his discourse, "the expression *to eat him*, even where the turn of his phrase" (it is said) "seems to invite him to use it;" for he does the same in what the author would call "the latter section." See verses 50, 51, 58, in which he employs the language, *eat of this bread*, "avoiding" (I might say) "the harsh expression," *eat me*. The difference of phraseology, therefore, is not so remarkably great as the doctor would induce his reader to believe.

"3. So long as Christ speaks of himself as the object of faith, under the image of a spiritual food, he represents this food as given by the Father (verses 32, 33, 39, 40, 44); but after verse 47 he speaks of the food, which he now describes, as to be given by *himself*. 'The bread *which I will give* is my flesh for the life of the world' (verse

52). 'How can *this man* give us his flesh to eat?' (verse 53). This marked difference in the *giver* of the two communications, proposed in the two divisions of the discourse, points out that a different *gift* is likewise promised. If faith is the gift in both, there is no ground for the distinction made in them; if there is a transition to a real eating, the whole is clear. While we consider Jesus Christ and his doctrine as the object of our faith, he is justly described as sent and presented to us by the Father; when we view him as giving his flesh to eat, it is by the precious bounty of his own love towards us." Here it may be replied, that whether the language of verse 51, "the bread which I will give is my flesh, which I will give for the life of the world," be explained of the atonement made by our Lord "in his own body on the tree," or in reference to the Romanist doctrine of the Real Presence in the Eucharist, the orthodox believer in the Trinity would hardly deny, that in either case the Father might well be said to be the giver, while the blessing is equally the gift of the Son. The "marked difference in the giver," therefore, is rather apparent than real, and no inference can be drawn from it in favour of " a different gift." Both the sacred persons give the same thing, which may therefore be stated as the gift of each. The author's language, " if faith is the gift in both communications," need hardly be animadverted on, as its inaccuracy is doubtless attributable to haste or inconsideration. Faith is the instrument by which the blessed donation is received No sound Protestant considers it as the gift itself.

"4. The difference here discernible between the givers is no less marked regarding the effects of the gift. To both are attributed the having everlasting life, and being raised up at the last day (verses 40, 44, 47, 52, 55, 59). But beyond this there is a marked distinction. In the first part of the discourse our blessed Saviour always speaks of our *coming to him* through the attraction or drawing of the Father (verses 35, 36, 44, 45). Now this expression is ever used when speaking of faith, to which we apply that part of his discourse. For example: '*Come unto me*, all you that labour' (Mat., xi., 28, cf. 27); '*Every one that cometh to me*, and heareth my words, and doeth them, I will show you to whom he is like' (Luke, vi., 47); 'Search the Scriptures, for you think in them to have everlasting life; and the same are they that give testimony of me; *and ye will not come to me*, that ye may have life' (John, v., 39, 40); 'If any man thirst, *let him come unto me* and drink. He that believeth in me,' &c. (vii., 37, 38), where the same image is used as in the first part of the discourse in the sixth chapter. Hence our Redeemer, at the conclusion of his discourse, says, 'But there are some of you that *believe not* ..... *therefore* did I say to you, *that no man can come unto me*, unless it be given him by the Father.' In this manner, the qualitics of the first method of receiving Christ's food, are precisely what we should expect if he treated of *belief.*

" But, after the place where we suppose the transition made, he speaks no longer of our coming to him, but of *our abiding in him, and he in us* (verses 57, 58). And this is a phrase which always intimates union *by love.* Thus (John, xiv., 23), 'If any one love me, he will keep my word, and my Father will love him, and we will come to him, and will make our abode with him.' In the 15th chapter (verses 4–9), the figure drawn from the necessity of the branches being united to the vine, gives the same result. 'As the branch cannot bear fruit of itself unless it abide in the vine, so neither can you unless *you abide in me*..... Abide in my love.' In the first Epistle of St. John, it is distinguished from faith as an effect from the cause. ' If that abide in you which you have heard from the beginning (the word of faith), you also shall abide in the Son and in the Father' (ii., 24). ' And now, little children, abide in him, that when he shall come we may have confidence, and not be confounded by him at his coming.' These words are more clearly explained in the 4th chapter (verses 16, 17), 'He that *abideth in charity, abideth in God, and God in him.* In this is the charity of God perfected within us, that we may have confidence in the day of judgment.' In addition, compare iii., 24; iv., 12, 13."

A plain man would think that "the difference

in the effects" cannot be very "marked," if such blessed consequences "as having everlasting life, and being raised up at the last day," are equally the result of each. Does Dr. Wiseman mean that "beyond THIS there is a marked distinction?" After having greatly excited our desire to know what this extraordinary distinction is, he tells us that "in the first part of the discourse," and elsewhere, our Saviour speaks of faith by the language *coming to him*, but after the supposed transition he does not speak of our *coming to*, but of our *abiding in* him, which intimates a union by love; to illustrate which he quotes several very apposite passages. Hence he concludes that "we have the effects of the doctrine inculcated after the 48th verse, given us quite different from those before rehearsed; and as the latter apply to *faith*, these are such as describe a union with Christ through *love*. Something, therefore, is here delivered or instituted, which tends to nourish and perfect this virtue, and not faith; the topic, therefore, is changed, and a transition has taken place. And what institution more suited to answer this end than the Blessed Eucharist? What could be more truly an instrument or means for our abiding in Christ and Christ in us?" He allows everlasting life to be the effect of faith, while, at the same time, he implies that a union with Christ by love, taught exclusively in the latter part of our Lord's discourse, is an effect "quite different" from and "beyond" it. Does he mean to teach us that *ev-*

erlasting life, the legitimate " effect" of faith, is attainable without a union with Christ, and that such union draws after it some other "effect," some higher benefit ? " Something," says he, " is here delivered or instituted, which tends to nourish and perfect this virtue (love), and not faith; the topic, therefore, is changed, and a transition has taken place." Undoubtedly something *is* here delivered and taught which *does* more directly tend to nourish and perfect love, and that something is " a true and lively faith," such as St. Paul describes in Hebrews, xi., 1, " which stirreth and worketh inwardly in the heart."* Why, then, should we suppose that the topic is changed ? Why is not the same living principle acting in all its holy energy upon the object which, most of all, is likely to call forth its efficiency, that is, the one sacrifice of Christ's precious body and blood, still to be regarded as the sole topic of our Lord's discourse throughout? There is evidently no reason for supposing a change of subject at all; but if there were, the newly-introduced topic would be, by the author's own showing, "a union with Christ by love." Any especial reference to the eucharist would be, I do not say inadmissible, but certainly unnecessary.

" 5. Our opponents suppose the phrases in the two portions of the discourse to be parallel, and to refer equally to faith. By this reasoning it fol-

* See *Homily* entitled " A short Declaration of the true, lively, and Christian Faith."

lows, that to eat his flesh (verses 54, 55, 56, 57) means the same as to possess the bread of life mentioned in the former section (verses 32, 33, 35)." And what does the author advance to show that it does not? "If," says he, "to feed on Christ mean to believe in Christ, then to eat the flesh of Christ (if the phrase has to be considered parallel) must signify to believe *in the flesh* of Christ. This is absurd: for the flesh and blood of Christ were not an object of faith to those who really sinned by believing him too literally to be only a man; nor can our belief in them be the source of eternal life."—P. 71. Now this is mere trifling; for no Protestant, in view of our Lord's discourse in the sixth chapter of St. John, ever identified "believing in the flesh of Christ" with believing him "too literally to be only a man:" and this the learned writer very well knew. The figment is original with Dr. Wiseman. The views implied or referred to in the remainder of the paragraph have already been considered, or shall be in the sequel.

The author, however, seems to think that all the nice distinctions which he has thus far made are either themselves of little importance (an opinion which I am sure will have the sanction of a large proportion of his most judicious readers), or else that, however great may be their absolute force when placed in the balance with the vast weight of what remains in the last place to be adduced, their comparative lightness will be perceived by every one. His sixth and concluding demonstration is introduced as follows:

"6. But all the differences which I have hitherto pointed out are mere *præludia* to the real, and, I trust, decisive examination of the point which yet remains." Notwithstanding the array of learning displayed in the argument thus introduced,* I shall venture to endeavour to follow the steps of the erudite author. If, perchance, something like a slip of the leader's foot should here and there be traced on the surface, let it not be forgotten that to stand firmly on such a ground requires all but a native right to the soil.

The argument is philological. The author inquires into the meaning of the phrase, "*to eat the flesh* of a person," in order to ascertain whether, when used by our Lord in this chapter, it can "be taken figuratively." And, after stating that the words must either be taken in their literal sense, or else in that figurative sense which usage has attached to them, he affirms, "that whether we examine the phraseology of the Bible, or the ordinary language of the people who still inhabit the same country, and have inherited the same ideas, or, in fine, the very language in which our Saviour addressed the Jews, we shall find the expres-

---

* The edition of Dr. Wiseman's book which I have made use of is that of Philadelphia, published by Eugene Cummiskey. If it should be thought advisable to issue another edition, it is hoped that attention will be paid to the Hebrew and Arabic quotations. The unfortunate misplacing of the words must have excited a smile in the author, if a copy of this should have fallen into his hands.

sion, *to eat the flesh* of a person, signifying invariably, when used metaphorically, to *attempt to do him some serious injury, principally by calumny or false accusation.* Such, therefore, was the *only* figurative meaning which the phrases could present to the audience at Capernaum."— P. 74.

He proceeds to show that the phrase in question is thus used in the Hebrew Bible, and occasionally in the New Testament; also, that the same metaphorical terms appear in the Koran and other Arabic writings; and that, in Latin, and, indeed, in most languages, calumny is expressed under the figure of gnawing, biting, &c. All this is, of course, unquestionable.

He then "passes to the language which our Saviour himself spoke" (or is generally supposed to have spoken), " and which was vernacular among the Jews whom he addressed." He shows that the same sort of figurative language appears in Chaldee and in Syriac. But it ought not to escape his reader's notice, that the usage in these languages, as appealed to by Dr. Wiseman, is not precisely parallel with the phrase *to eat the flesh of one*, the original words being אכל קרצי די, and invariably meaning, *to eat bits* or *morsels of one*, not בסרא, *flesh*; in the words of WINER, whom he quotes, "alicujus *frusta* comedere," " die *Stücken* jemandes fressen." Still, though there is some difference in the words, the expression no doubt means to calumniate.

Here it may be remarked, in passing, that Dr. Wiseman's assertion, "that the name διάβολος (devil) is translated throughout the Syriac version of the New Testament by אכל קרצא, *ochel kartzo, the eater of flesh*" (*a bit*), is strangely incorrect. The author makes the same statement in his Lectures on the Principal Doctrines and Practices of the Catholic Church. The fact stands thus: The word διάβολος occurs in the New Testament thirty-eight times, in nineteen of which the Syriac version does not employ this expression, but four others. Once, Luke, viii., 12, it uses a compound term, denoting *enemy*; once, Acts, x., 38, the word for *wicked* or *evil*; three times, Rev., xii., 9, 12; xx., 2, a word synonymous with *impostor, deceiver*; and fourteen times, Matt., xiii., 39. Luke, iv., 5. John, vi., 70; xiii., 2. 1 Tim., iii., 6, 7. 2 Tim., ii., 26. Heb., ii., 14. James, iv., 7. 1 Pet., v., 8. 1 John, iii., 8, three times, and verse 10, the word *Satan*. The representation of Dr. Wiseman is true only of the other nineteen places in which διάβολος is found. This should make the reader cautious how he receives the doctor's statements of this kind without examination; for it must be admitted that, in this instance, there is an unpardonable want of accuracy, to say the least.*

* Since writing the above, the author's reply to certain English controversial publications has come into my hands. In the fourth Lecture of his original work, p. 145, in endeavouring to show that the term *flesh* cannot be used in our Lord's discourse to denote "the literal sense," as "*letter* is in some instances," he adds, "especially in

In the third Lecture he proceeds to show that the Jews regarded drinking blood as highly crim-

a chapter wherein it has been used *twenty* times in its ordinary meaning." One of his opponents, Dr. Turton, mentions the fact that the word had been employed before the 63d verse but *five* times by our Lord, and *once* by the Jews. Dr. Wiseman endeavours to vindicate himself from the charge of "extraordinary exaggeration" by saying, that by the expression "twenty times, he meant, as every one not engaged in controversy would have understood, *often.*"—Reply, p. 19. The reader will determine whether such looseness is allowable in a writer engaged in philological discussion. The remark, in a note, that he "had accurately stated, in its proper place, the number of times the phrase was used, while here the subject came in indirectly," is inadmissible, as the frequency of the use of the term was evidently intended to have a bearing on his argument.

Another representation of this author is of so extraordinary a nature that I forbear any attempt to characterize it. In his second lecture, p. 87, 88, he had quoted from Tittmann's Meletemata Sacra. Dr. Turton objected to his application of this writer's language. In reply, after speaking of "the Regius Professor's either blundering or unfair comment" as "a curious specimen of the learning of a controversialist," our author remarks as follows : "But this is not the most curious part of this extraordinary proceeding. I quoted the *Meletemata Sacra*. I suppose the learned professor was unacquainted with the work; so, like a good controversialist—certainly not like a good scholar—he goes to another work of Tittmann's, and from that attempts to confute me. This is his commentary on *St. John*. Now in this, Tittman, being a Protestant, interrupts our Lord's discourse Protestantly, and says, 'apud nostros,' that is, among German Protestants, there is no doubt that no reference is here intended to the Blessed Sacrament. But how, I ask, does this opinion of Tittmann's invalidate his statement, that it is not by the *usus loquendi* that this interpretation is attained, which is all that I quoted him for? Suppose that the learned German admits *other* ways of arriving at an explanation of phrases; this does not prove my allegation of him false, when I cited him to contradict Mr. Townsend's assertion, that the Protestant interpretation *is* based on the *usus loquendi*. The words from the *Meletemata Sacra* are as clear as those from the Commentary; nor will any quotation from the latter obscure or invalidate the former."—*Reply*, &c., p. 186.

The scholar will know what to think of this. The merely general

inal, and eating human flesh as implying " the most dreadful curse which the Almighty could inflict." Hence he infers that our Saviour cannot be supposed to " have clothed doctrines no ways repulsive under imagery drawn from such an odious source; that nothing but the absolute necessity of using such phrases could justify the recurrence to them; and, therefore, that he used them because it was his wish to teach the doctrine which they literally convey, that of the Real Presence."—P. 97, 98.

The proposition on which the argument is based is undoubtedly true. The Hebrews, in common with a large proportion of mankind, cherished the feeling ascribed to them; but the inference founded upon it is by no means a necessary result. The figure of eating is suggested by the miracle performed the day before; it is continued, most probably, in consequence of the captious Jews having referred to the manna, as miraculously given by Moses for the support of their forefathers;

reader will hardly believe me when I assure him that the Meletemata Sacra is the same book as the Commentary—that the very words "apud nostros" (to which the learned author adds, "nec apud verum doctum esse potest," showing that he had no idea of limiting the doubt to " German Protestants") occur on p. 276, which are here professedly drawn from " another work"—and, moreover, that the edition quoted by Wiseman, in his second Lecture, is that of Leipsic, 1816, now lying before me, the title-page of which is as follows: " Caroli Christiani Tittmanni, Theol. Doct., &c., &c., Meletemata Sacra sive Commentarius Exegetico-Critico-Dogmaticus in Evangelium Joannis." Comment is superfluous.—Tittmann's book is well worth the attention of theological students. It is learned, sensible, and pious.

and the particular phraseology evidently repeats and amplifies the language of their own objection, as I have just stated. The expressions, *to eat me*, and *to eat my flesh and drink my blood*, contain identically the same thought; and if the one would necessarily be revolting to a Jew, as implying what is disgusting and criminal, so also would the other, as intimating to his mind the idea of cannibalism. And yet it is allowed that this might be, and it is quite evident that it is, employed in the figurative meaning, which those who dissent from the doctrine of the Real Presence would attach to the other. (See p. 70, bot.) The argument of the author is vastly stronger against the whole doctrine of transubstantiation than it is against a figurative use of such phraseology. The inference naturally to be drawn, when language is employed which "orders a person to commit what he" not only "deems, but really is, a heinous crime," is this, that such language must not be understood literally; whereas, according to Wiseman's system, our Lord's hearers, and his followers in every age, are actually required to do what is considered so exceedingly criminal. Surely, in avoiding an imaginary Scylla, the lecturer has plunged into a real Charybdis.

I proceed now to what is called "the most important proof." This is stated to be "the direct testimony of those addressed (as) to how they understood our Saviour, and his warrant for the correctness of their interpretation."—P. 99, 100. The former remark proves nothing more than that the Jews misunderstood him, as they had often done before; the latter would settle the point if it could be admitted, but, unfortunately, it is not true. Before I examine the grounds alleged by the author in defence of it, I cannot but express my wonder that he should close some observations tending merely to show how our Lord's hearers understood him, with the language, "Thus far, then, we have the strongest testimony we can require to our Saviour's having passed in his discourse to the literal eating of his flesh" (p. 102), when the testimony does not purpose to prove anything beyond this single point, that he had been literally understood by them. Their misapprehension is represented as the real meaning!

He asserts, " That whenever our Lord's hearers found difficulties or raised objections to his words, from taking them in their literal sense, while he intended them to be taken figuratively, his constant practice was to explain them instantly in a figurative manner,* even though no great error could result from their being misunderstood."— P. 103. He adduces several instances (although Matt., xix., 24, and John, viii., 21, are very little to the point), and undoubtedly our Lord very often did explain his meaning. But to infer from ordinary practice a universal, invariable usage, without a single exception, cannot be admitted. There

* He means, that our Lord made his hearers know that the language was figurative, and communicated his thought in proper terms.

might be strong reasons, and sometimes not ascertainable by us, for omitting explanation in particular cases, which would not ordinarily apply. The conclusion drawn is universal in its application, while the induction of particulars intended to sustain it is, at the most, only general. Admitting that our Lord adopted the method of instructing by parable in order to make the best and most lasting impression, it is impossible to deny that he explained himself more clearly to his disciples than he did to certain others. " Unto you it is given to know the mysteries of the kingdom of God, but unto them that are without all these things are done in parables. Without a parable spake he not unto them, and when they were alone he expounded all things to his disciples."—Mark, iv., 11, 34. In Matt., xvi., 4, indignant at the people's continued want of faith, notwithstanding the most direct evidence, he declares that no sign should be given them but that of Jonas the prophet, without explaining wherein it consisted ; and in xxi., 27, he expressly refuses to " tell by what authority" he acted. The cases in John, ii., 19, 20, and in iv., 10–15, where his figurative language is misunderstood, while nothing explanatory is added, are examined by the author ; but he does in express words, and with marked inconsistency, abandon his own theory, and contradict the affirmation with which he set out. In the words just quoted he states that " our Lord's *constant practice was to explain;*" on page 107, " from examples" alleged by him, he "deduces a *very certain corollary or canon,* that *whenever* our Saviour's expressions were erroneously taken in their literal sense, and he meant them to be figurative, it was *his constant practice instantly to explain himself,* and let his audience *understand* that his words were to be taken figuratively." Let us turn now to page 117 and 119. "I have never said that our Saviour was bound to answer the objections of the Jews ; but I have examined only his practice *when he did answer or explain,* and have found that his conduct was precisely that of an honest and upright teacher, *who corrected mistakes,** and enforced his doctrines without fear. But in the case of John, ii., *he deems it right to give no answer at all,* and the passage only proves that our Saviour *sometimes declined answering an objection*" (he should have said explaining a figure). " To the instance," in John, iv., " I will briefly reply, that our Saviour *declines answering*" the Samaritan woman's " *difficulty at all.*" Really, either bonus dormitat Homerus noster, or he presumes very much on the lethargic disposition of his hearers and readers. The avowed abandonment of his own principle entirely precludes the necessity of a more minute examination of his remark.

The author's fourth and last Lecture remains to be considered. In it he continues his argument by

---

* Does the doctor mean to imply, that when he did not correct mistakes, that is, when he did not answer or explain, his conduct was not precisely that of an honest and upright teacher ?

an "analysis of our Saviour's answer to the Jews and their incredulity," and also by examining his conduct to his disciples and apostles. After answering "objections to" what he is pleased to call "the Catholic interpretation of the chapter," he closes the subject.—P. 123, *seq.*

In reviewing the author's course of remark, it is impossible to avoid the difficulty of prolixity, which most probably the reader, in common with myself, has already felt in this discussion. It is necessary to present the argument, if not in all cases as fully as it is stated in the author's work, yet always sufficiently so to be clearly understood, and afterward to say what may be proper in reply. What in the original Lecture may be comprehended within very narrow limits, may require a considerable space in order to be suitably examined. I shall endeavour to be brief, unless at the expense of necessary indefiniteness and obscurity.

1. The first argument is founded on "the double form, negative and positive," in which the "precept" that contains the "doctrine" is conveyed (verses 53, 54), which he compares with "the words of St. Mark, 'He that believeth and is baptized shall be saved, but he that believeth not shall be condemned,'" xvi., 16. Hence he is led to make 'two reflections:" first, "the beautiful similarity of form with which we find the two principal sacraments of the Christian religion inculcated, if with the Catholic Church we suppose the words of St. John to refer to the Eucharist;" and, secondly

"the clearness of the expression in St. Mark, and the absolute absence of comprehensibility in that of St. John, the moment we take it in the Protestant sense." Neither of these reflections contains any argument. The latter is an instance of that begging of the question which appears not unfrequently in the work, and, consequently, does not require notice; and the former only proves that the form of expression in the two cases is similar. To infer from this that the words under consideration were intended to teach the doctrine of the Real Presence is ridiculous. All that the comparison of the two places shows is this, that in giving instructions, or laying down laws with their sanctions, our Lord and his Apostles sometimes adopt the negative and the positive forms in connexion. Among numerous instances, it may be sufficient to select two. "Whosoever shall confess me before men, him will I confess also before my Father which is in heaven; but whosoever shall deny me before men, him will I also deny before my Father which is in heaven."—Matt., x., 32, 33. "He that believeth on the Son hath everlasting life; and he that believeth not the Son shall not see life, but the wrath of God abideth on him."—John, iii., 36.

2. Our search for argument in the next paragraph is equally fruitless. Indeed, the writer here shows a rashness in exposing his Church to attack which is really amazing. "In these words, our Lord makes a distinction between eating his body and drinking his blood; a distinction without any

real signification or force, if he be not speaking of the Real Presence; for to partake of the blood of Christ by faith adds nothing to the idea of partaking of his body." I will not lay any stress on the fact, that in this discourse our Lord never employs the word " body" at all (although, in reference to the interpretation which explains it exclusively of the eucharist, it is not unimportant), for its use by our author may be a mere inadvertence. But if there really be such a *significant and forcible distinction*, and if the command to *drink the blood* is as unlimited as that to *eat the flesh*, both being intended to be understood literally, on what ground of Scripture or reason do Dr. Wiseman and his coadjutors withhold *the blood* from the people, that very blood which has a *distinctive force and significancy?* So far as anything like argument in the passage may be discerned, the answer is simply what has been before said, namely, that the two phrases *eating the flesh* and *drinking the blood* are employed emphatically, both conveying the idea of a thorough reception, and, by consequence, a most intimate union.

3. The third argument is founded partly on the supposition that our Saviour meant to answer an objection, and partly on the asseveration expressed by the words verily, verily. This, it is said, is unwarrantable, " if he meant to be understood only of a belief in his death, to which doctrine the objection of the Jews was not directed." Certainly it was not. Neither is it said by orthodox Protestants

that a mere belief in his death is what our Lord intended; but a belief in it as an atoning sacrifice for sin, and such a belief as recognises its value and necessity, giving to the believer a vital union with the sacred object of his faith, and leading him to a correspondent life of obedience. This is what the hearers had no conception of, and therefore they express not so much their "objection to the doctrine," as their inability to understand the meaning of the words by which it was conveyed. "How can this man give us his flesh to eat?" is equivalent to saying, "this is unintelligible and absurd." The "strong asseveration" is not, as Dr. Wiseman supposes, "an answer to a difficulty," but a repetition of the announcement before made, and it is imbodied in the very words of the cavillers. Whether the supposition, that he thus " insists on the necessity of believing in him" in such a way as has been just stated, " is to imagine him acting wantonly and insincerely with their judgment and feelings whom he had undertaken to instruct," as the author affirms, is a point which shall be afterward considered.

4. The next remark relates to the expression in verse 55, "my flesh is meat indeed, and my blood is drink indeed," or "truly meat and truly drink," which he regards as "confirming the literal meaning of the words." He acknowledges "that the word *truly** is spoken, not merely of identity of

---

* Whether we adopt the reading ἀληθής or ἀληθῶς, the sense remains the same.

things, but also of their qualities, so that Christ calls himself the true vine when he only spake in parables." But he asks, "While the Jews understood our Saviour to speak of *really* intending to give them his flesh to eat, if they were wrong, can we suppose him to answer them by saying, that his flesh was *really* meat? Or can we, under these circumstances, imagine him to use the word at all, and that twice and emphatically, unless he wished to be taken literally?" This is nothing more than a repetition of what he had said in the former paragraph, and might be dismissed without farther remark. Yet it may be well to note, that the same sort of language is employed in a previous part of the chapter, where no one thinks of a literal interpretation. See verses 32-35, and compare Luke, xvi., 11. "If ye have not been faithful in the unrighteous mammon, who will commit to your trust the *true?*" The use of the word does not prove that it must be taken literally, but, rather, that it is intended to impress and inculcate some most important consideration

5. The last "confirmation" of the literal sense is found in "the harsh expression (verse 57),'he that eateth *me.*'" It is left to make its own impression on the reader, whom it is sufficient to remind, that wisdom, personified under the image of a female, employs the same language: "They that *eat me* shall yet be hungry, and they that *drink me* shall yet be thirsty."—Eccles., xxiv., 21.

Dr. Wiseman, having thus satisfied himself that

"almost in every phrase this reply of our Saviour affords a strong confirmation of the Catholic doctrine," proceeds " to consider the effects which this answer produced upon his hearers."

1. " Instead of removing their previous difficulties, it manifestly confirmed them." They regarded his " proposition as harsh and revolting, and could not bear to listen to it. They were more convinced than ever that he spoke of the real manducation of his flesh."—All this only shows that they persisted in misunderstanding his meaning.

2. " Jesus answered these murmurs by the words, Doth this scandalize you ? If, then, ye shall see the Son of Man ascend up where he was before! (verses 61, 62)." According to Dr. Wiseman, the object of this reply of our Lord " is to refer his auditors to a great and striking proof which he was to give that he had divine authority to teach, and that his words were to be believed, whatever difficulties they might present." And this view, he thinks, is illustrated by John, i., 50, 51, and Matt., xxvi., 63, 64. He " considers the appeal to his ascension in the sixth chapter of St. John" as equivalent to the inquiry, " Would you not receive my word after such a confirmation ?" But the force of this argument depends wholly on the author's interpretation of the question; whereas the more natural sense, and which is better sustained by the context, is that which makes our Lord imply the absurdity of the literal meaning, by appealing to the manifest unreasonableness and self-

contradiction of literally eating his flesh and drinking his blood, after his body should have been removed from them into heaven.

3. "The consequence of this conference is, that 'many of his disciples went back, and walked no more with him' (verse 67). Can we suppose that Jesus would have allowed things to come to this extremity, that he would cast away forever *many* of his disciples, when an explanation in two words would have saved them? And yet even this did he, if the Protestant interpretation of his discourse be true." Here, again, the lecturer assumes, *more suo*, an honest and candid disposition in the disciples who relapsed. But let us suppose that they were governed by worldly and merely prudential considerations, and we may easily account for their going back, as "they had no root in themselves." They may have sought the prophet of Nazareth, "not because they saw the miracles" and felt their force, "but because they did eat of the loaves and were filled," and hoped to eat again. This representation of their character will be more particularly illustrated, and its correctness evinced, in a subsequent part of the Essay.

4. Christ's conduct towards the twelve is alleged as "affording additional assurance of the correctness of the literal interpretation of his discourse. He asks them, after the departure of other disciples, 'Will ye also go?' Whoever reads the answer which Peter gives to this touching 1estion must be convinced that the Apostles were

manifestly perplexed as to the nature of their divine Master's intentions. For Peter does not even allude to the doctrines taught, but throws himself entirely upon his belief in our Saviour's authority, and answers accordingly: 'Lord, to whom shall we go? thou hast the words of eternal life.'— (Verse 69.) Now when we consider that to them it was given to know the mysteries of the kingdom of God, it must appear extraordinary that even to them he should not have condescended to give any explanation of this singular enigma, which Protestants suppose him to have been uttering. By one only hypothesis can we solve this difficulty, by acknowledging that they had really understood him right, but that he spoke of a mystery which only required faith—and *that* they had clearly professed through Peter—but which could not receive any explanation, so as to bring it within the comprehension of reason."

To reply as nearly as possible in the writer's own words, I would say: "When we consider that to the Apostles it was given to know the mysteries of the kingdom of God,* it must appear extraordinary that even to them he should not have condescended to give any" illustration of, or to remove any difficulty relating to, "this singular mystery, which" Romanists "suppose him to have been uttering." For, allowing that it "cannot receive any explanation so as to bring it within the comprehension of reason," yet, as it is apparently

* Luke, viii., 10.

at variance with reason, and certainly contradicted by the testimony of four of the five senses, it is impossible to " solve the difficulty" pressed upon us by the want of any attempt to elucidate the doctrine, or to lessen the perplexity which must have embarrassed the minds of the Apostles, except "by acknowledging that" the exposition suggested by our Lord, when he said, " the words that I speak unto you are spirit, and they are life," is the only true one, and that the phrases *eating his flesh* and *drinking his blood* are not to be understood of " a real manducation of his body," but of a spiritual union with him by means of a living faith.

The author proceeds: " In order to condense and sum up the arguments which I have hitherto brought in favour of the Catholic dogma, I will propose a very simple hypothesis, and deduce them all from its solution." That is to say, he intends to state a hypothesis, which is to be very simple; to solve it, which implies that, notwithstanding its great simplicity, it contains some difficulty which must be removed; and this being done, the arguments hitherto alleged will be condensed and summed up. Although I freely confess myself at a loss to comprehend the full meaning of all this, yet, as it is evident that he means to do something, which, if done, would make all his previous labour unnecessary, I cannot but express my regret that he should not have solved this very simple hypothesis and made his deductions therefrom before, as it seems really unkind, with such a purpose and ability, to have given his hearers and readers so much useless trouble, as a proper examination of the preceding part of his work demands.

He then, with great truth and beauty, delineates our Saviour's character as independent, and, at the same time, humble; as bold, yet gentle; firm, yet meek; exhibiting to all successive teachers the most perfect pattern for imitation. This delineation he brings to bear on the Protestant exposition of his discourse in John, vi., in order to show that such an exposition is utterly at variance with this character. As the author's representation either imbodies part of what he had before said, or assumes what he cannot prove, it might be passed over. But for the sake of general readers, who cannot be expected to examine minutely into the correctness of all his statements, I feel compelled to make one or two remarks. " The Protestant" is represented as supposing the Saviour " to undertake to expound one of his most beautiful and consoling doctrines to a crowd of ardent and enthusiastic hearers, who had just before followed him into the wilderness, and fasted three days in order to listen to his instructions."— P. 134. Now all this is a figment of the author's imagination. The Protestant supposes no such thing. It is the learned doctor who confounds two distinct facts; namely, the feeding mentioned in Matt., xv., 32–38, and Mark, viii., 2–9, of the four thousand, of whom it is said, that they had been "with Jesus three days, and had nothing to eat," with the feeding of "five thousand men, besides women and children" (making, in all probability, nearly as many more), narrated in Matt., xiv., 16-21, and John, vi., 5-13, which miracle had been performed some time before. Those were not the religious men who had come from far, had fasted three days, and were likely to faint by the way if dismissed. And it is extraordinary that such a mistake should appear in a "theological course of lectures several times delivered in the English college at Rome," and, in order to "do ample justice to the line of argument pursued," not only repeatedly delivered, but published, and, of course, revised and prepared for the press. A careful perusal of this very chapter might have pointed out this mistake; for John, vi., 22-29, tells us, that "the people came to Capernaum, seeking for Jesus *the day following*" the miraculous feeding: consequently, they had enjoyed a good meal *the day before* the discourse was addressed to them. If they were the "ardent and enthusiastic hearers" which it is all-important to the argument to represent them, how is it that "the model of all meekness, condescension, and sweetness" opens his discourse to them with a charge of selfishness and irreligious indifference, introduced, too, with a strong asseveration? "Verily, verily I say unto you, ye seek me because ye did eat of the loaves, and were filled." Does he ever begin to address well-disposed hearers in such language as this?

How is it that these enthusiastic admirers of Jesus, hanging as it were upon his lips, demand a sign, and tell him that Moses wrought a miracle of long continuance in giving their fathers the manna? Is this the way of enthusiastic admirers? How is it that he who "needed not that any should testify, for he knew what was in man,"* solemnly declared to these *ardent and enthusiastic hearers*, " I say unto you that ye have seen me and believe not?" verse 37. How is it that he plainly enough intimates to them that they were not under the Father's influence? verses 44, 45. How is it that these "*docile disciples*" murmured at him because he said "I am the bread that came down from heaven?" verse 41. If such is the author's hypothesis, it is, with all its supposed simplicity, encumbered by difficulties which neither he nor any other ingenious solver of doubts can expound. The truth is, that he has entirely misapprehended the character of these men. He has confounded them with others who appear to have been of very different disposition, by identifying two distinct and independent facts; and when he says that "one word of explanation would have saved them from their apostacy," he asserts what he cannot know, and what is utterly irreconcilable with the facts of the case. His argument is wholly founded in error. Had he properly investigated and reflected on these points, he might have spared himself and his readers the

* John, ii., 25.

questions, whether "this conduct of Jesus could win the affections of the infidel?" Whether "such conduct is a model for imitation?" Whether "any Protestant bishop would instruct his clergymen to act thus in reference to children who should misunderstand their catechism?" p. 136. All this seems intended *ad captandum*. The thoughtful examiner must feel that it assumes the thing to be proved.

And so also does Mr. COLERIDGE, in the quotation from his "Aids to Reflection," with which Dr. Wiseman closes his lecture. "After which time many of (Christ's) disciples, who had been eyewitnesses of his mighty miracles, who had heard the sublime morality of his Sermon on the Mount, had glorified God for the wisdom which they had heard, and had been prepared to acknowledge the Christ, went back and walked no more with him! What every parent, every humane preceptor would do when a child had misunderstood a metaphor or epilogue in a literal sense, we all know. But the meek and merciful Jesus suffered many of his disciples to fall off from eternal life, when to retain them he had only to say, Oh, ye simple ones, why are ye offended? my words, indeed, sound strange; but I mean no more than what you have often and often heard from me before with delight and entire acquiescence! Credat Judæus: non ego." The learned and profound author assumes, respecting these disciples, what is not susceptible of proof.

How does he know that they " had heard the sublime morality of the Sermon on the Mount, had glorified God for its wisdom, and been prepared to acknowledge the Christ ?" How does he know that they would have been so easily retained? How does he know that these disciples were not merely external hangers-on to the supposed Messiah, from whom they had hoped to receive honours and dignities in his secular kingdom? How does he know that they were not men filled with the spirit of this world, without any taste for an inward union in sentiment, affection, and whole character with the pure and holy one whom they professed to regard as their master? To assume all that he says, merely because the persons in question are called disciples, is too large a demand to be readily complied with by those who bear in mind that Judas was a disciple, and a chosen apostle too, and that yet " the meek and merciful Jesus" himself does not scruple to call him " a devil." In fact, with all due, and, therefore, with very great respect for the philosophic thinker and poet, I am constrained to be of the opinion that, in this representation, the force of his eloquence and imagination predominates over that of his logic.

The view taken of the character of these men by St. Augustin and Chrysostom is much more in accordance with the real facts. " They were far away from the bread from heaven ; neither did they know what hungering for it meant. They had the jaws of the heart languid; with open ears, they were nevertheless deaf; they were seeing, and yet they remained blind. For that bread requires the hunger of the inner man." Such is the representation of the deeply religious African bishop.* The golden-mouthed patriarch of Constaǹtinople also remarks, with great truth, that "the obscurity of what is said excites the attention of the hearer;" and hence he infers most correctly, that this ought not to give offence, but rather to lead to inquiry. "But now they go away. For if they had believed him to be the prophet, they would necessarily have believed his declarations; *so that the stumbling-block lay in their folly, and not in the obscurity of what was said.*"† And afterward he contrasts the humble fidelity of true disciples with the querulous disposition of these multitudes, who exclaim, this is a harsh doctrine, and consequently depart from him.

As might be supposed, the author proceeds to show "how beautifully the Catholic interpretation suits the well-known character of Jesus." As the whole is nothing but a graphical description of a

* Isti a pane de cœlo longe erant, nec eum esurire noverant. Fauces cordis languidas habebant; auribus apertis surdi erant; videbant, et cœci stabant. Panis quippe iste interioris hominis quærit esuriem. In Joan., Tract. xxvi., Opera, tom. iii., p. 357.

† Ὥστε τῆς ἐκείνων ἀνόιας τὸ σκάνδαλον ἦν, ὀυ τῆς ἀπορίας τῶν λεγομένων. In Joan., Hom. xlvi., Al. xlv., Opera, edit. Bened. Venet., 1741, tom. viii., p. 271.

hypothetical case, any review of it is wholly unnecessary

The last subject proposed for examination relates to " the different arguments brought by Protestants to prove that our Lord's discourse cannot be referred to the eucharist." These will be considered in a subsequent part of this Essay, to the subject of which they most properly belong.

PART II.
ANALYSIS AND EXPOSITION OF THE DISCOURSE.

Having sufficiently examined most of the leading arguments intended to support Dr. Wiseman's view of this discourse of our Lord, I proceed to consider its general scope and meaning.

I have already stated the circumstances that gave occasion to the discourse, and the wonder expressed by the multitude on finding Jesus at Capernaum. Discerning their real character, he accuses them of unworthy and selfish motives, and exhorts them to seek earnestly the spiritual and everlasting food which could be imparted only by himself, whose authority God had indubitably attested. "Verily, verily, I say unto you, ye seek me, not because ye saw the miracles, but because ye did eat of the loaves and were filled. Work not for the meat which perisheth, but for that meat which endureth unto everlasting life, which the Son of Man will give unto you; for him hath God the Father sealed," verses 26, 27. The reader cannot fail to observe that the figure selected by our Lord whereby to convey his exhortation is taken from the food miraculously supplied on the preceding day. This is agreeable to his usual manner. We have a striking illustration of this in his conversation with the Samaritan woman at Jacob's Well, whom he had asked for a drink, and to whom he immediately after recommends the blessings of the Spirit under the figure of living or running water.* Another, equally strong, may be found in his illustration of the deplorable condition of the Jews of his day, under the idea of an evil spirit taking his seven companions, and returning with vastly increased force to the residence from which he had been expelled. This illustration is doubtless suggested by his having just before relieved a blind and dumb demoniac, and vindicated himself from the calumnious charge of his virulent opposers.† And, as he seizes on late or passing events to supply suitable figures, so does he occasionally employ the very language of his hearers to convey his own thoughts, the manner and tone giving them perspicuity, impression, and vitality.‡

Attention to our Lord's usage in these respects may throw light on some parts of this discourse. When his hearers, in evident allusion to his words, inquire of him, "What must we do that we may *work* the *works* of God?" he immediately replies, "This is the *work* of God, that ye believe on him whom he hath sent," verses 28, 29. The great work, the work required by God and acceptable to him, the work which is the true principle and

---

* John iv., 10, 14.   † Matt., xii, 43–45; 22, *seq*.
‡ See John, ix., 40, 41; and compare Luke, xx., 16, with Matt xxi., 41.

germ, as it were, of all other works, is a right faith in Christ. This is the introductory proposition laid down by him in this important discourse. It is first stated in figurative language, and then in literal. And it is never lost sight of; it is repeated over and over again, with the same change of expression. Thus, he promises blessings to the believer when he says of him in figure, "he that *cometh* to me shall never hunger," and adds, in proper terms, "he that *believeth* on me shall never thirst," verse 35; meaning, shall be abundantly supplied with the Spirit.* Thus he says of the believer, using the same figure, "him that *cometh* unto me I will in no wise cast out," verse 37; and again, without a figure, that "every one that *believeth* on him he will raise up at the last day," verse 40; and again, with the same figure, that the Father's influence is necessary to produce this faith, "no man can *come* to me except the *Father* which hath sent me *draw* him," verse 44; and that the attentive and docile are divinely taught and do so believe, "they shall be all *taught of God*: every one, therefore, that *hath heard and learned* of the Father *cometh* unto me," verse 45; and, once more, solemnly pledges the full blessings of the Gospel to all such: "Verily, verily, I say unto you, *he that believeth* on me hath everlasting life," verse 47. It is essentially important to regard this as the main principle advanced and urged.

* Compare iv., 13, 14; vii., 37, 38

In what manner, now, do these Jews receive our Lord's doctrine respecting this "work of God," that is faith? Do they show themselves, according to Mr. Coleridge's representation of their character, as disposed to glorify God for the wisdom which they had heard, and prepared to acknowledge, "this is indeed the Christ?" Do they manifest the docile temper of the "child," to whom he compares them? Do they drink in his words with delight, as we might expect such "ardent and enthusiastic hearers," as Dr. Wiseman represents them, would do? On the contrary, although they had seen him perform the most amazing miracle, by which their own wants had been abundantly supplied,* like their perverse and faithless ancestors in the desert, they disregard it, and demand another, wishing, perhaps, for a continual supply, such as that afforded to their fathers by the manna, and setting the miracle of Moses in contradistinction to that of Christ. "They said, therefore, unto him, What sign showest thou, then, that we may see, and believe thee? what dost thou work? Our fathers did eat manna in the desert, as it is written, he gave them bread from heaven to eat," verses 30, 31. Perhaps, too, they meant to imply, that if Jesus were the true Mes-

* Lücke's supposition, that those who required a miracle were not present at the miraculous feeding the day before, and had only heard of it, and seem to have doubted it, is wholly at variance with probability, and disproved by the circumstances of the occasion. See his Commentar über die Schriften des Evangelisten Johannis, vol. ii., p. 176.

siah, he ought, like his predecessor, to cause manna to be rained from heaven. The passage referred to is Ps. lxxviii., 24, 25, where the Hebrew has דְּגַן שָׁמַיִם corn (food) of heaven, לֶחֶם אַבִּירִים bread of mighty ones (angels), and the Septuagint, ἄρτον οὐρανοῦ ἔδωκεν αὐτοῖς· ἄρτον ἀγγέλων ἔφαγεν ἄνθρωπος: he gave them bread of heaven; bread of angels man did eat. The words used in the Gospel, ἐκ τοῦ οὐρανοῦ, are susceptible of the same sense, as the substantive with the preposition is sometimes employed instead of the adjective. Thus, for instance, in Luke, xi., 13, we have ὁ πατὴρ ὁ ἐξ οὐρανοῦ, for heavenly Father, and in 2 Cor., v., 2, τὸ οἰκητήριον ἡμῶν τὸ ἐξ οὐρανοῦ, for heavenly habitation. But although the idea of heavenly food, very excellent and miraculous in character, is of course conveyed, the words seem to be chosen in order to express also the source from which Christ himself, the true bread, the living antitype of the manna, came; and the language in Exod., xvi., 4, both in the Hebrew and Septuagint, is similar: "I will rain for you bread *from heaven*," מִן הַשָּׁמָיִם, ἄρτους ἐκ τοῦ οὐρανοῦ. The ὁ καταβαίνων, in verse 33, should be translated in connexion with ἄρτος, the bread which cometh down, and so the hearers understood it, for they immediately ask for such bread, verse 34. The present, in verses 33 and 50, expresses the inherent character of this food; it is heavenly, and from heaven it always comes. When our Lord speaks of himself as having come from heaven, St. John employs the aorist, καταβάς. See verses 41, 51 with which compare καταβέβηκα in verses 38, 42.

To this demand of the Jews, most unreasonable in itself, and clearly indicative of want of right perception and feeling, our Lord replies with earnestness, that the true bread from heaven was not given by Moses, but by his own Father, that it is himself, the manna being only a material symbol and figure of the spiritual reality, and that this is intended, not like the ancient miraculously communicated food, to assist in sustaining the present life of a few, but to afford eternal life to the whole world. Having no internal character adapted to a perception of his meaning, and dwelling on the gross idea of corporeal food to be imparted daily by their Messiah, whereby present life should be sustained without toil, they exclaim, " Lord, *always* give us this bread," verses 32–34. He immediately corrects their sensual error by declaring that the bread just spoken of is himself, adding also a promise to every one that believeth on him, verse 35. Then he repeats what he had before plainly implied, that, although they had seen him in his character as a divine teacher, and had been eyewitnesses of his miracles,* yet they still remained unbelieving, verse 36; a statement quite irreconcilable with the representation of their character which has been already referred to. He proceeds to state an important truth, to which

---

* This, though not asserted, is evidently implied. Compare similar language in Matt., xxiii., 39: "Ye shall not see me henceforth."

afterward also he calls their attention (verses 44, 45), namely, that it is only through the Father's influence that any are enabled truly to believe in him, thereby intimating the danger of forfeiting by prejudice and passion all reasonable expectation of securing it, verse 37. Now he assumes the prerogatives of the divine Messiah, and affirms that he will not reject the believer, but will raise him up at the last day, and this in accordance with the will of the Father, to accomplish which he came down from heaven, verses 38–40. Were these statements of Christ received with the docility of children, to say nothing of the ardour of enthusiastic disciples? The next verses inform us that they "murmured at him," and were not prepared to admit his Messiahship. "Is not this Jesus, the son of Joseph, whose father and mother we know? How is it, then, that he saith, I came down from heaven?" (verses 41, 42). No wonder that the divine teacher, after checking their murmurs, insists on the necessity of the Father's grace, and of docility in the subject. 'No one can believe in me except the Father draw him; all such are taught by him, and are diligent and docile pupils, instructed by the invisible, yet ever-present and influencing God.' Verses 43–46.

The assertion made in the former part of verse 44 is simply this, that no one can believe in Christ without the influence of the Father, and the next verse shows that such effective influence is imparted to those only who attend and learn. Ἐλκυσῃ by no means implies an irresistible operation. The use of words, which in their own nature denote force, merely in a moral and limited sense adapted to the character of the object acted on, is very common in Scripture. Thus, we have ἀναγκάζω and βιάζομαι employed in the sense of inducing, urging, pressing, where no sensible expositor would think of any stronger meaning; as in Matt., xiv., 22; Mark, vi., 45; Luke, xiv., 23; Acts, xxviii., 19; Matt., xi., 12; Luke, xvi., 16. And so ἑλκύω, which with ἕλκω often conveys the idea of dragging, is here used of a moral influence, which may be resisted and counteracted. Compare xii., 32, which undoubtedly expresses the thought, that the Gospel system of Christ crucified would attract multitudes. See, also, James i., 14, where ἐξελκόμενος is used of a person being *drawn away* by sinful passion, irresistibility being out of the question. And, lastly, compare the use of εἵλκυσαν με, in Cant., i., 4, (3), immediately followed by ὀπίσω σου—δραμοῦμεν, let them *draw me*, we *will run* after them.

Here I must be allowed to interrupt the general current of the discourse, by calling the attention of the reader to the 37th verse: "All that the Father giveth me, shall (will) come to me; and him that cometh to me I will in no wise cast out." The reason why such shall not be rejected immediately follows; it is the Father's will, to accomplish which Christ came down from Heaven, 38–40. Notwithstanding the use of the neuter πᾶν persons are certainly meant, as is proved by the nature of the subject, and the masculine τὸν ἐρχόμενον that follows. This usage is not uncommon with St. John, and is found also in other writers. Thus, we have in i., 12, τὰ ἴδια and οἱ ἴδιοι, nearly, if not quite, synonymous; in xvii., 2, ἵνα πᾶν ὅ δέδωκας αὐτῷ, δώσῃ αὐτοῖς; and in 1 John, v., 4, 5, πᾶν τὸ γεγεννημένον ἐκ τοῦ Θεοῦ νικᾷ τὸν κόσμον, is followed by τίς ἐστιν ὁ νικῶν τὸν κόσμον εἰ μὴ ὁ πιστεύων. Virgil also employs the neuter to designate persons:

> "Et quidquid tecum invalidum metuensque pericli est,
> Delige, et his habeant terris, sine, mœnia fessi."
> *Æneid*, v., 716, 717.

When our Lord says, "all that the Father giveth me will come to me," he means to teach us, that those who truly believe on him are given him by the Father, that is, are led to believe by the Father's influence. It may not be unworthy of remark, that δίδωσί is present. Compare verse 32. All is the Father's gift. He impresses this consideration, implying, of course, the danger of provoking the Father to withhold it. The perfect in verse 39 expresses the accomplishment of belief by the Father's influence; as if he had said "This is the Father's will, that all who have become true believers through his influence should be raised to life." With this view of the much litigated words, "the Father giveth," the next verse coincides, the phrases, *seeing the Son* and *believing on him*, being substituted for them, and expressing, also, the necessity of using all suitable means to acquire the truth. Compare verse 36, which is addressed to such as did not believe, although they had seen him. The idea is yet more clearly developed in verses 44, 45, which insist on the necessity of the Father's influence and of our docility. *He that heareth and learneth* of *the Father* is substituted for *whom the Father giveth.*

A comparison of other places in this Gospel, where the same or similar language occurs, is altogether favourable to this view. Thus, in x., 29, " the Father who *gave them* to me," that is, ' who so influenced them by his grace as to induce them to believe on me, and thus to become mine.' See, also, the texts in the 17th chapter, which are all susceptible of a clear exposition in the same way, verses 2, 6, 9, 11 (if δυς be the true reading, which is better supported by internal evidence than external), 12, 24. The same thought occurs, also, in vi., 65, although the form of expression is somewhat varied: " No one can come to me except it be *given him* of my Father ;" in other words, ' to become mine by a true faith requires the gracious influence of the Father.' Compare the language of xix., 11: " Thou couldst have no power against me, except it were *given thee* from above," that is, ' thou canst only act under divine permission." Also, iii., 27, " A man can receive nothing, except it were *given him* from Heaven."

If it should be said that, inasmuch as coming to Christ is identical with believing on him, the view now given makes our Lord, in verse 37, utter the truism, 'All that the Father, by his grace, induces to believe on me will believe on me,' the answer is, that the first clause need not, in all cases, comprehend *all* that the next asserts. The phrase, "giveth to me," may occasionally bear a more limited sense, equivalent to 'properly influences for me,' while at others it includes the effect of such influence, namely, right faith. Such limitations of the ordinary meaning of a word, or, on the other hand, some accession to it, is by no means of unfrequent occurrence in Scripture.

I will only add, that a careful attention to the wide range of meaning allowed by Hebrew usage to the word *give* will tend not a little to remove any difficulty which the reader may feel in the statements here made.

The divine teacher now resumes the leading topic of his discourse, which he introduces with the strongest asseveration, verse 47. There is a close connexion between this verse and the preceding. The great object of faith is he who, "being in the bosom of the Father" (i., 18), and having seen him and been most intimately associated with him, and having also been sent by him from heaven with the fullest authority and power, is consequently able to give eternal life. He is the food that imparts and sustains life; the life which alone is worthy of the name (48). 'Your fathers ate the manna in the desert, yet they died; however extraordinary and excellent the food thus communicated, it was incompetent to perpetuate even their animal life; whereas the antitype of the manna, the spiritual food which has no association with earth, but descends from its own heaven, imparts and preserves a life which is beyond the influence of death, verses 49, 50. I am that life-giving, life-sustaining, and never-failing food, having come down from heaven;' verse 51, former part. The participle "*living*" in this place does undoubtedly convey the idea of everlasting, indestructible, and heavenly, in opposition to what is temporary, decaying, and earthly. Permanency, possessing the principle of life, is its usual meaning. Still, as it is undeniable that our Lord speaks of himself as the giver and sustainer of spiritual life (verses 33, 35, 50), it is best to take the word in its most comprehensive sense. Ὁ ἐκ τοῦ οὐρανοῦ καταβάς, may refer to ἐγώ or to ὁ ἄρτος. I have endeavoured to adapt the translation to the grammatical ambiguity of the original. The meaning of the whole clause will remain the same.

I come now to that portion of our Saviour's discourse which requires the most careful examination. After telling his hearers that the food of which he has been speaking is himself, he proceeds to say, more particularly in the latter part of verse 51, that it is his flesh, which he will give for the life of the world. A declaration seemingly so extraordinary, and to them unintelligible, became the occasion of excitement and disputation; and, attaching no other meaning to his words than a carnal and literal one, such as their gross views of the supply of bodily food which the Messiah was to furnish would naturally suggest, they speak of it contemptuously, and as a palpable impossibility: "How can this man give us his flesh to eat?" verses 51, 52. The Master enjoins the necessity of their doing what they regarded as absurd and impracticable, in order to obtain spiritual life; he enjoins it with a strong asseveration, with particularity of expression, employing the words "drink the blood" as well as "eat the flesh of the Son of Man." To those who so do, he promises a joyful resurrection; he speaks of this food and drink as the best and truest; of the one who uses it as intimately united with him, as partaking of life by* him as he does by* the Father; and concludes by characterizing it as having come down from heaven, and by contrasting its effects in conveying spiritual and everlasting life with those of the manna, on which their deceased ancestors had lived for a time in the desert, verses 53–58. What means he by this eating his flesh and drinking his blood?

* The usual meaning of διὰ with an accusative is, *on account of*, with a genitive *by*. (See, for an instance of each usage, Heb., ii., 10.) Still it is acknowledged by the best grammarians, that in the New Testament διὰ is sometimes (though very seldom) used with the accusative in the sense of means; cause, object, and means being so intimately allied. See Winer's Grammatik N. T., p. 324, 339. The above translation is therefore sanctioned by occasional usage, and is to be preferred, because it produces a meaning best adapted to the context and subject.

The expression, "And, moreover,* the bread which I will give is my flesh, which I will give for the life of the world," cannot be explained merely of Christ's devoting himself, consecrating his whole earthly life to man's welfare. The word *flesh* is never used in this sense, neither can it be said, in accordance with it, "the bread which I *will* give is my flesh, which I *will* give." This denotes a future act, whereas the consecration referred to had been already made in a good degree, and was still in progress.

Neither is it correct to say, that having spoken in the preceding part of his discourse simply of his doctrine, our Lord now introduces another distinct and additional idea, representing his death as what was to give life unto the world. For what is this sentiment but a part of his doctrine, a very prominent and important part, and implied in what he had already said? Such a distinction and supposed transition are without evidence.

Are we, then, to explain this part of the discourse solely or principally in reference to the eucharist, and to interpret the phrases "eat the flesh and drink the blood" in accordance with the doctrine of transubstantiation, or in reference to the symbols of bread and wine representing the real body and blood of the Redeemer? There are difficulties in this view, some of which cannot be removed, and of which it is necessary to take notice.

1. It might be said, that the word here used is

* I have employed these words to convey the force of καί—δέ.

flesh, while *body* is always employed elsewhere, as in the words of the institution as given by the evangelists and St. Paul.* If our Lord intended here a particular reference to the eucharistic body or symbol, it would seem reasonable to expect him to have used the same word on both occasions. To this it may be replied, that such arguments are not of much weight, because, as either word is well adapted to express the thought intended, the choice of either may have been rather circumstantial than necessary. This is true; and yet the reader must feel that if the eucharistic food be meant, the sense would have been clearer if the word *body* had been employed as elsewhere.

2. On this theory it is not easy to explain the language, "I will give," in verse 51. This cannot be interpreted of the eucharist, for Christ's flesh or body was not then given. The words of the institution, "Which is given—which is shed,"† have, indeed, been alleged to prove that the giving and the shedding, that is, the offering made by Christ when he gave himself to be crucified, and allowed his blood to be poured out as a sacrifice and libation for human guilt, was made at that time and in that very act. But this is plainly at variance with repeated declarations of the Apostles, that the offering of the body of Jesus Christ was made once for all by his death upon the cross.‡

* Matt., xxvi., 26. Mark, xiv., 22. Luke, xxii., 19. 1 Cor., xi., 24.
† Luke, xxii., 19, 20.
‡ See, among other places, Heb., vii., 27; ix., 25–28; x., 10, 12, 14. 1 Pet., ii., 24.

The use of the present τὸ διδόμενον, τὸ ἐκχυνόμενον, το κλώμενον (1 Cor., xi., 24), is easily explained, as the Saviour represents before the eyes of his Apostles a symbol of what was so very soon to take place. Such language is very common. Thus we read, " The hour is coming, and *now is*, when the dead shall hear the voice of the Son of God."* Whether this be understood of a literal, or, more correctly, of a moral resurrection, does not affect its application to the case in hand. Of the same kind is our Lord's language, " The hour *is come* that the Son of Man should be glorified ;" " *now is* the judgment of this world."† The proximity or certainty of what is stated is the ground of the usage. And on the same principle, what is still future is sometimes spoken of as past, as is often the case in prophecy. Thus, also, our Lord, in his last prayer before his passion, speaks as if his whole atoning work on earth were completed, as if he had already risen, and was going to his Father. The language is particularly worthy of notice: "I *have finished* the work which thou gavest me to do; and *now I am no more in the world:* while I *was with them in the world* I kept them."‡ When, therefore, our Lord employs the present in the eucharistic institution, he does so, not because he means to teach us that his sacrifice was then offered, not that his body was then given, his blood then shed; but because this was so soon to take place, that it is in his mind as if it

* John, v., 25.   † xii., 23, 31.   ‡ xvii., 4, 11, 12.

were present, though, strictly speaking, it was only symbolized by the celebration.

It is certain, then, that the words "I will give," cannot be explained of the eucharist. They must be understood of Christ's voluntary sacrifice on the cross, as the same verb is employed in other places. Thus, for instance, it is said, "The Son of Man came *to give* his life a ransom for many —he *gave* himself a ransom for all—who *gave* himself for our sins—who *gave* himself for us."* This is the only meaning that accords with usage and harmonizes with the context. If, then, the language of verse 51 is to be explained of something different from the eucharist, it follows necessarily that the eating and drinking afterward mentioned must also relate to something different, for the connexion is so intimate as to compel us to understand both of the same general topic.

3. On the theory by which this passage is expounded of the eucharist, it is not easy to explain the fact, that St. John, in his Gospel, gives no account of the institution. It will, doubtless, be said, and for this very reason he introduces this discourse, that he may impress its necessity. And even Bishop BEVERIDGE, who does not understand this discourse as intended directly of the eucharist, expresses the opinion, "That St. John, having recorded words so very like to those in the institution of that holy sacrament, did not think it neces-

* Matt., xx., 28. Mark, x., 45. 1 Tim., ii., 6. Gal., i., 4. Tit., ii., 14.

sary to describe, as all the other evangelists did, the institution of his Last Supper."* Still it appears unnatural to speak in direct reference to an institution which our Lord himself originated, and which, in this respect, is different from baptism, and to speak of its use as necessary in order to obtain Christian privileges, without taking any notice of its establishment. It is certain that those who derived their knowledge solely from this Gospel could not so have understood the discourse; this is true, also, of the original hearers. And, on the other hand, if this part of our Lord's discourse was intended to refer primarily to the eucharist, it is somewhat extraordinary that the other evangelists should have given their readers no account of it. The institution would so naturally have suggested the discourse, that it is not easy on this theory to explain the omission.

4. Closely connected with this difficulty is another, which Dr. Wiseman "thinks the most favourite reason given for not understanding this discourse of the eucharist," namely, "that it was not yet instituted."† And SHERLOCK,‡ as quoted by him, notes this as "the only objection he knows against so expounding" it. It is surprising that the

---

* Sermons, London, 1708, vol. v., p. 314. † Page 139.

‡ The author of the discourse from which Dr. Wiseman makes an extract is Dean SHERLOCK, not the bishop, who was his son. This is a mere inadvertence. In the same way, the Sacred Theory of the Earth, which was written by Dr. THOMAS BURNET, has often been ascribed to the bishop, whose Christian name was GILBERT, and sometimes printed as his.

knowledge of so distinguished a divine should on this point have been so limited. We are told by the reverend author that "there are several answers to this" objection. They are given by Dr. Wiseman, with some original "remarks" and "illustrations."

Sherlock replies to the objection, that " our Saviour said a great many things to the Jews in his sermons which neither they nor his own disciples could understand when they were spoken, though his disciples understood them after he was risen." Dr. Wiseman illustrates this by reminding the reader " of the distinction between *comprehending* and *understanding*, the latter referring to the meaning of the words, the former to the nature of the doctrine." That Christ's flesh and blood were to be eaten and drunk the hearers could readily understand, although " they could not comprehend how this was to be effected."*

This is certainly true, and the distinction is important. It is in the highest degree reasonable that the understanding should give its full assent to the truth of a proposition, or acquiesce in the obligation of a precept, although it may not comprehend the nature of the one nor the manner of complying with the other. One thing it perceives and knows, namely, that in the one case some truth is contained, in the other some act is enjoined. This perception and knowledge are founded on the previously established authority of him

* Page 139.

with whom the proposition or precept originates. On this principle, therefore, we should be justified in maintaining that there is sound mathematical truth in some proposition of Newton's Principia, even if we could not comprehend its meaning. We merely confess our ignorance and acknowledge his authority. And thus, if it be sufficiently proved that, in the case under consideration, the thing intended is the eating and drinking in the eucharist, the bare fact that our Lord's original hearers could not have comprehended the nature of the thing, and "how it was effected," is not a valid objection. They could readily understand that something in reference to himself was to be done; and reason as well as faith required them not only to acquiesce in the proposition, but to resolve to do the thing, and to wait patiently until they should be instructed in its nature and manner.

The principle, then, on which the dean's observation is founded is not only the basis of sound and acceptable faith, but it is an essential element of reason, the highest degree of both being always in perfect harmony. Our Saviour's discourses contain frequent illustrations of it. When, however, Dr. Wiseman "gives" as "one, his conversation with Nicodemus," which, he says, "took place before baptism was instituted, and yet the necessity of it is there declared," adding that "no one has ever thought of denying that the regeneration there mentioned referred to baptism, on the ground that this sacrament had not been instituted,"* he is singularly unfortunate in his selection. He assumes what, beyond all doubt, he could not prove. Yet even if his assumption were allowed, the cases would not be relevant. I will not urge that the practice of baptizing proselytes to Judaism was then in general use. This might be questioned; although, on the theory which wholly denies its use antecedent to the coming of John, it is difficult to account for the question of the delegation sent to him from Jerusalem: " Why baptizest thou, then, if thou be not the Christ, nor Elias, neither the prophet ?"† The language seems to imply, that, had he avowed himself to be any one of these personages, they would not have been surprised at his baptizing, and consequently implies, also, that they were familiar with the usage as a ceremony of initiation. Waiving all this, however, it is a matter of fact that John, as the precursor of the Messiah, had been publicly baptizing, and that crowds had flocked to him from Judea and Jerusalem. The use of water, then, in admitting to discipleship in the doctrine of the prophetic Elias, must necessarily have been known to Nicodemus, and he could not have failed to apply the well-known fact as explanatory of our Lord's language. But it is not necessary to take this view. It is in the highest degree probable that Christ's baptism was in use before the conversation held with Nicodemus. The first direct mention that is made of our Lord's

* Page 140.   † John, i., 25.

baptizing is, indeed, in the verse that follows the account of this interview; but the apparently incidental manner in which the practice is introduced makes it extremely probable that he had already instituted, or, which is equivalent, sanctioned the rite: " After these things came Jesus and his disciples into the land of Judea; and there he tarried with them and baptized."—John, iii., 22: compare verse 26; iv., 1. Those places show the practice immediately or shortly after the interview with the Jewish ruler. Before it, Christ had publicly avowed himself to be the Messiah, by clearing his father's house of profanation, by a symbolical prediction of his death and resurrection, by working miracles so remarkable, either in number or kind, or both (ii., 22; iii., 2), as to induce a member of the Sanhedrim to show him the respect of a visit, and to recognise him as a divine teacher. All this implies that he spent some time in the great capital, and must have elicited a considerable degree of public attention. As an effect of his actions and instructions, "many believed on his name;" and the probability is in favour of the opinion, that such persons made the same public profession of their faith as those did who became his disciples after the interview; in other words, that they received his baptism. When, therefore, Dr. Wiseman asserts that "the discourse in the sixth chapter of St. John stands in the same relation to the institution of the eucharist as the conference with Nicodemus does to the institution of baptism,"* he makes a statement which is entirely gratuitous, and without even the shadow of a proof.

Still, while the illustration of Wiseman must be rejected, the principle of Sherlock is freely admitted. Our Saviour's precept might have a subsequent institution in view, and relate to something hereafter to be done. Let us now examine if such is the fact.

On this supposition, it will be difficult to explain satisfactorily why our Lord did not openly and plainly announce his intention of instituting the eucharist, in which either his flesh and blood, or the symbols of them, should be eaten and drunk. It is true that, on the theory of transubstantiation, such a declaration would not have removed the harshness of the precept in the opinion of the hearers, but it would at least have given them a clear idea of his meaning. On the Protestant theory of the eucharist, it would at once have removed the whole difficulty. The strength of this consideration must, of course, be increased in the minds of those who, with Dr. Wiseman and Mr. Coleridge, have taken a favourable view of the docility and religious honesty of the party addressed, from whom it is not to be supposed that such information would be withheld.

Farther, the general tenor of the discourse shows, that when our Lord urges on his hearers the duty and necessity of "eating his flesh and

* Page 141.

drinking his blood, he means that the persons addressed should themselves, without delay, do the thing required. It is evident that the whole discourse preserves a proper unity of subject, and that verses 48–58 inclusive are indissolubly connected. Notwithstanding the several phrases employed in verses 53–58, the subject required to be eaten is the same throughout. But the language in verse 58, " This is that bread which came down from heaven: not as your fathers did eat the manna and are dead, he that eateth of this bread shall live forever," necessarily refers us back to that of verses 31–33: " Our fathers did eat the manna, as it is written, he gave them bread from heaven to eat—verily, verily, I say unto you, my Father giveth you the true bread from heaven, for the bread of God is he that cometh down from heaven and giveth life unto the world;" and both are most clearly connected with the very first direction, "labour (or work) for that meat which endureth unto everlasting life, which the Son of Man shall give unto you," verse 27. It is quite evident, then, that our Lord is not asseverating in his most solemn manner the necessity, in order to secure union with him and a glorious resurrection, of obeying a law which was not to be plainly promulgated until a year after,* but is urging an immediate compliance with the command which introduces his discourse.

5. The effects of obedience and disobedience,

* Compare vi., 4, vii., 1, 2, and Matt., xxvi., 19, 26.

as stated by Christ, do not harmonize with the interpretation which refers this passage principally or wholly* to the eucharist. "If any man eat of this bread he shall live forever—whoso eateth my flesh and drinketh my blood hath eternal life, shall live forever, dwelleth in me and I in him, and I will raise him up at the last day. Verily, verily, I say unto you, except ye eat the flesh and drink the blood of the Son of Man, ye have no life in you." I do not attach much importance to the fact that all this is said absolutely. I am willing to grant that such language might be employed of what has been called "sacramental feeding," while the condition that the eating and drinking be rightly and worthily done, that is, with suitable dispositions on the part of the communicant, is implied. Absolute declarations, when the subjects of them are in their very nature conditional, and also shown to be so by the analogy of God's dealings, are often made in Scripture. But so solemn a warning, implying the most serious threat and such glorious promises, are never represented in the New Testament as the result of neglecting or

---

* I do not acquiesce in the inference as Dr. Wiseman has stated it: "precludes the possibility *of any reference* to the eucharist." Neither do the divines he refers to maintain this. Indeed, the very language of Beveridge which he quotes shows the contrary. "It is not the sacramental, but spiritual eating his body and blood our Saviour here speaks of. I mean, our Saviour hath no *particular reference* in this place to the representatives of his body and blood in the sacrament, but only to the spiritual feeding upon him by faith, whether *in* or out of the sacrament." It is not easy to defend the doctor's candour and perspicacity both.

complying with any one positive institution. Certainly, this is so in reference to the other sacrament. He never read, "He that is baptized shall be saved," but "he that *believeth and is baptized*," while we do read, "he that *believeth not* shall be damned," and "*whosoever shall call upon the name of the Lord* shall be saved ;"* and it is particularly worthy of notice, that when baptism is mentioned as saving, cleansing, forgiving, there is generally, if not always, some word or phrase added, expressive of internal sanctification. Thus, when Ananias requires Saul to "arise and be baptized, and wash away his sins," he adds, "calling on the name of the Lord," which implies the necessity of prayer as well as of outward profession.† And when St. Paul speaks of Christ "having purified his Church by the washing (or bath, λουτρῷ) of water," he immediately adds, "through the word,"‡ implying the efficacy of the "truth"§ in producing the result. St. Peter, also, when he speaks of "baptism saving us," is careful to guard against the error of attaching this important result to the outward act, and therefore explains it to be "not the putting away the filth of the flesh, but the answer of a good conscience towards God," adding, also, "by the resurrection of Jesus Christ."‖ Here inward purity is presumed to exist along with the outward act, and Christ's resurrection is repre-

---

* Mark, xvi., 16.   Acts, ii., 21.   Rom., x., 13.
† Acts, xxii., 16.   ‡ Eph., v., 27.   § John, xvii., 17.
‖ Pet., iii., 21.

sented as the procuring cause of the blessing. And, lastly, when the apostle contrasts outward circumcision in the flesh with that not made with hands, it is evident that with the external sign he conjoins the thing signified, "the putting off the body of flesh, the being buried along with Christ, and being raised with him to a new and holy life." To suppose, therefore, that such "exceeding great and precious promises" as those before us are annexed to the sacramental feeding, however explicable such a representation might be with the necessary condition implied, is not in harmony with the usage of the New Testament Scriptures.

What, then, it may be asked, is the meaning of the words in question? I answer, the same as had already been conveyed by the phrases before employed; namely, the duty and rewards of a living faith in the Redeemer, with the fuller and more distinct development, however, than had been before made of the atoning sacrifice which was to be effected by his death, and the necessity of this faith acting on it, in order to secure the pardon of sin, the mystical union of the believer with his Lord, and, by consequence, his attainment of present spiritual life, of future resurrection, and of eternal happiness. The exercise of such a faith is what is meant by "eating the flesh and drinking the blood of the Son of Man," by whatever means of grace it may act, whether they were in existence and operation at the time when the discourse was uttered, or were subsequently developed or established.

This view of our Lord's meaning is drawn from the occasion and whole tenor of the discourse as already presented. He begins by urging faith; he replies to the querulous objections of his opponents by inculcating faith; he proceeds by repeatedly stating the necessity of the Father's influence to produce faith; and, after he has finished his discourse, and corrected the gross error of some of his hearers, he introduces the same fundamental principle of faith, as effected by the Father's influence. "There are some of you that *believe* not; for Jesus knew from the beginning who they were that *believed* not; and he said, therefore said I unto you, that no man can *come unto* me, except it were given unto me of my Father," verses 64, 65. And, moreover, to the question, "Will ye also go away?" the honest, the truly "ardent and enthusiastic" Peter responds in his master's own strain, "We *believe* and are sure that thou art the Christ, the Son of the living God," verse 69. The verbal difficulties which can set aside such an interpretation, sustained by the facts that gave occasion to the discourse, by its whole train and tenor, and by the leading idea pervading the mind of both teacher and disciple after it had been delivered, ought to be not only weighty, but overwhelming.

The profound and universally-acknowledged "judicious" Hooker lays down a principle of interpretation, the truth of which is founded in the nature of the mind and the purpose of language:

"I hold it for a most infallible rule in expositions of sacred Scripture, that where a literal construction will stand, the farthest from the letter is commonly the worst."* Nothing can be more true. But let us not lose sight of the condition: " where a literal construction will stand;" that is, where it not only makes a good sense, but the sense best adapted to the scope of the author, most in harmony with his ordinary manner and the general object which he has in view. Now I deny that this is the case in the present instance. It is of little consequence to say that the sacramental exposition gives the plain and literal sense of the word. This does not prove it to be true: it only imposes on those who object to it the obligation of showing that the literal sense cannot be the correct one; which I conceive has often been done. The literal exposition throughout necessarily results in the doctrine of a real corporeal presence. If the flesh and the blood are both to be understood literally of the Saviour's bodily substance, which is to be incorporated with the body of the worshipper, his bodily substance must be present whether by con- or tran-substantiation. But it may not be amiss to remind the advocates of the most literal sense, that if they will be true to their principle, they must allow that the words cannot prove the real presence of anything else than the bodily substance. I do not deny that where Christ's body

* Eccles. Polity, book v , § 59

is, there also is his soul, and there his divinity in an especial manner; but this might be denied by one who, at the same time, justly claimed to be a most rigid adherent of the literal sense. Figure of some sort, and in some degree, must be admitted by all. Either the phrase "flesh and blood" is a synecdoche, a part for the whole; or it is a metaphor, the thing signified for the sign; or the whole clause, which speaks of eating the one and drinking the other, is tropical. It is idle to object to the view before given because it is figurative. No interpretation can be entirely literal.

Sherlock objects, that if the expressions are to be explained "of feeding on Christ by faith or believing, his disciples could understand this no better than that which expounds it of the Lord's Supper. It is plain they did not, and I know not how they could. For to call bare believing in Christ, eating his flesh and drinking his blood, is so remote from all propriety of speaking, and so unknown in all languages, that to this day those who understand nothing more by it but believing in Christ are able to give no tolerable account of the reason of the expression."*

Dr. Wiseman asserts, that even if the phrase "to eat the Messiah" could mean "to receive and embrace him, the expression to eat the flesh of the Messiah is totally different, and that the least departure from established phraseology plunges us in obscurity and nonsense."†

* Pages 132 133. † Page 96

In reply to the last-mentioned writer, it is sufficient to say, that words and phrases often take their determinate meaning from the particular occasion and circumstances which give rise to their use, by which, also, their meaning is often modified; so that all "obscurity" is thereby removed. Our author does himself recognise the principle here stated, and I am happy to confirm its correctness by his authority. "Philology is not conducted" merely "by taking the abstract meaning of words and applying them to any passage, but by studying them as used in peculiar circumstances." —P. 127. The case before us proves the truth of this; for it is undeniable that some of the best critics and commentators, both of ancient and modern times, have agreed in giving to "the expressions, to eat the flesh and drink the blood of the Messiah," a meaning which Dr. Wiseman says implies a "departure from established phraseology," without either "obscurity" or "nonsense." There is, in truth, neither nonsense in the meaning, nor necessary obscurity in the language which conveys it. The *bread* to be eaten is expressly declared by our Saviour, in verse 51, to be his *flesh*. It is evident, therefore, that eating the bread, in verses 48, 50, 51, is identical with eating the flesh. Whatever the one means the other must also mean. The language, "Except ye eat," &c., in verses 53–56, is suggested by that in which the objection is couched, in verse 52, "How can this man give us his flesh to eat?" to which the words "drink the blood" are added simply to particularize, so as to denote a thorough partaking, and the whole is an amplification of the thought before expressed, in verses 50, 51, namely, the "eating of the bread that cometh down from heaven." And in verses 56, 57, 58, the phrases, "eateth my flesh and drinketh my blood—eateth me—eateth of this bread," are manifestly identical in meaning. The amplification may be illustrated by Ephes., v., 30, where the apostle, after stating of true Christians, that they "are members of Christ's body," immediately adds, in order to show more particularly the intimacy of the union intended, " of his flesh and of his bones." (Compare the language of the Israelites to David : "We are thy bone and thy flesh."*) To suppose that he intends to denote a personal identity thereby would be a monstrous extravagance, unsupported by Scripture, and directly tending to a species of Pantheism; and, moreover, contrary to the comparison taken from the marriage relation which gives occasion to the language.

It is quite superfluous to show, not only that our Lord frequently draws his figures from what has just occurred or is passing at the time, but, also, that he often clothes his thoughts in language taken from the lips of his hearers, employing their very words in a sense different from that intended by them. See John, ix., 40, 41. Matt., xii., 48, 49; xxiii., 31, 32; and compare Ezek., xvi., 45. In

* 2 Sam., v., 1.

fact, such a modification of the meaning of words is common with all speakers, and particularly in colloquial and popular discourse; and it rarely gives any difficulty to the honest, candid hearer. I am not aware that an instance of the word ἡμέρα, in the metonymical sense of *judgment* in which it is used in 1 Cor., iv., 3, has ever been adduced from any Greek writer; and yet no one is in danger of mistaking the sense, which is necessarily suggested by the context. It is neither a Cilicism nor a Hebraism, but an elliptical manner of employing a word expressive of time to designate the action then to be done, the nature of the action having been already sufficiently brought before the reader. On the same principle, we have in our Lord's discourse an amplification of the idea which he had already plainly and repeatedly stated. If some of his hearers misunderstood him, the fault lay with themselves, and is not attributable to any necessary obscurity in the language.

With regard to Dean Sherlock's objection, which is represented as "certainly satisfactory," the first remark to be made relates to a part of the language chosen to convey it. He speaks of "bare believing, nothing more than believing." Whatever may have been his design in selecting these expressions, it is impossible to mistake their tendency. This, evidently, is to fill the reader's mind with the impression that the sense objected to is inadequate to the dignity of the subject, too low and feeble for the solemnity of the manner and the force of the language. But if, more in accordance with the general representations of Scripture, we consider the faith thus enjoined, not as "*bare believing*," but as "believing *with the heart unto righteousness*,"* as the faith "which *worketh by love*,"† which "is *the substance of things hoped for and the evidence of things not seen*,"‡ as that which, by its living and active energy, unites to the true and life-giving head, producing a spiritual union and blessed incorporation with him as members of his mystical body, and, consequently, bringing along with it the participation of Christ here and the full enjoyment of him hereafter; then it cannot be questioned, that we have a sense sufficiently elevated for any occasion and any allowable warmth of language.

He says, moreover, that the expressions could have been understood of faith in Christ no better than of the Lord's Supper. This is mere assertion. And it can by no means be admitted, as faith is the leading thought which pervades the whole previous part of the discourse, whereas not a syllable had been said of the Lord's Supper. The former idea might and ought to have been the prominent one in their minds; the latter could not by any possibility have been conceived. We must not take up the expressions of eating and drinking as if they were isolated. We are compelled to examine them in connexion with and by

* Rom., x., 10.   † Gal., v., 6.   ‡ Heb., xi., 1.

the aid of the context, and are therefore compelled to acknowledge, that while the idea of faith naturally suggests itself, that of sacramental eating in the Lord's Supper must have been derived from subsequent instruction.

But the advocates of the theory which interprets our Lord's language of faith rather than of the Lord's Supper, "are able to give no tolerable account of the reason of the expression."

It is granted that the expressions are unusually strong, and that the figure is developed with extraordinary boldness. At the same time, it is contended that it is the same sort of figure as had all along been employed, and to which the occasion gave rise. The words imbodying the one thought are varied; and this, as has already been said, because our Lord adopts the very terms of his opponents, and because the general figure having been already repeatedly employed, these terms are an amplification well fitted to express the closeness of the union intended. The increased strength and boldness of the terms will appear natural to all who patiently attend to the circumstances. They are also in analogy with other Scriptural representations, of which I shall adduce a single instance. St. Paul, delineating the inward working of the natural mind, when reason is acting on the subject of religious obligation, and the conscience is in some measure alive to a regard to it, while, at the same time, the grace of the Gospel is wanting, uses the language, "*I consent* unto the law that it is good."* This simply expresses acquiescence in its excellence. But afterward, becoming more warmed with the subject, and desiring to state as fully as possible the completeness of this acquiescence of reason and conscience, he employs a stronger term, "συνήδομαι, *I delight in*, or, *am pleased with*, the law of God, after the inner man."† The expressions, "eat the flesh and drink the blood of the Son of Man," when considered in relation to the language "eat me," are similar to the latter word of St. Paul in relation to the former. In each case, both expressions designate the same thing, the one being only more fervid and energetic than the other.

It is hardly necessary to remark, that words denoting food and beverage, and freely partaking thereof, have in all ages and nations been employed to signify an ardent attention to learning, a reception of doctrine, particularly when it engages the whole mind, and interests the affections. This is admitted on all hands, and Dr. Wiseman, among other writers, has given some very apposite quotations to this effect.‡ The reason of the figure is evident. As the food is taken into the system, combines with the substance, nourishes and strengthens it, and thus becomes a natural cause of its continued vitality; so does the learning or the doctrine embraced influence the intellectual or moral character of the recipient. Hence he is commonly said to *imbibe* its excellence, to *taste*

* Rom., vii., 16. † Verse 22 ‡ Pages 60–63.

and enjoy its sweetness, to *devour* the truth with greediness, or to *swallow* error with avidity. Perhaps no people were more accustomed to an extreme use of this figure than the Hebrews. It occurs very often in the New Testament, and abounds in the Old. Illustration may be unnecessary, yet I will cite a few passages. " If any man hear my voice, I will *sup* with him and he with me:* I have *fed* you with *milk*, and not with *meat:*† I have *eaten* my honeycomb with my honey: I have *drunk* my wine with my milk: *eat*, O friends, *drink*, yea, *drink abundantly*, O beloved:‡ the Lord of Hosts shall make a *feast of fat things*, a *feast of wines on the lees; of fat things full of marrow.*"§ The same class of expressions is used to convey the idea of *enjoying* and *delighting in* anything. Thus, for instance, "Thy words were found and I did *eat* them, and thy word was unto me the *joy and rejoicing* of my heart."‖ Also, for a hearty reception in contradistinction to an unwillingness to see and admit the truth: "Thou son of man, be not thou rebellious like that rebellious house; open thy mouth, and *eat* that I give thee. *Eat* that thou findest, *eat* this roll. So I opened my mouth, and he caused me to *eat* that roll; and he said unto me, son of man, *cause thy belly to eat, and fill thy bowels* with this roll that I give thee. Then did *I eat it; and it was in my mouth as honey for sweetness.*"¶ Here the figure of eating is carried

* Rev., iii., 30   † 1 Cor., iii., 2.   ‡ Sol. Song, v., 1.
§ Isa., xxv., 6.   ‖ Jer., xv., 16.   ¶ Ezek., ii., 8; iii., 1-3.

out; the food is to be taken freely, so as to pervade the whole system; it also communicates pleasure to the prophet who obeys the command. Wisdom personified employs similar language: " They that *eat me* shall yet be hungry, and they that *drink me* shall yet be thirsty,"* that is, shall be desirous of more. Attention to these particulars may assist in showing the connexion between certain Hebrew words expressive of *feeding* and *satisfaction*, as רָעָה and רָצָה, and may also explain the fact that the former is used to denote *association* and *union*.

The same figure is employed by later Jewish writers. Thus the Rabbis say, that "every eating and drinking mentioned in the book of Ecclesiastes refers to the law and to good works;"† and MAIMONIDES employs similar language when he speaks of " filling the stomach with bread and meat," while he means to express the idea of " knowing what is lawful or unlawful."‡ Passages have also been cited from the Talmud, in illustration of our Lord's language, and to them I must now request the reader's attention, and the more particularly, as they are commented on by Dr. Wiseman, who quotes them from Lightfoot.

As the portion of the Talmud in connexion with which the passages occur is curious, and may

* Ecclus., xxiv., 21.
† This is a quotation from the Midrash Koheleth, and has been repeatedly cited by the commentators.
‡ Jad Hazakah, Grounds of the Law, chap. iv., *ad fin.*, fol. 7, vol. i., Amsterdam edition.

serve to illustrate opinions of the ancient Jews in reference to certain prophecies respecting the Messiah, which their descendants of the Middle Ages and since have generally applied to some other object, and chiefly to the body of the nation personified, I shall not hesitate to make a larger quotation than is absolutely necessary merely to throw light on the phraseology in St. John. I shall give as literal a translation as the idioms of the two languages will allow, inserting the original words no farther than is required, in order to show the allusions of the Talmudist, and what may be called his play upon the words cited from Scripture. He has just given certain comments of the Rabbis on Jer., xxx., 6, a small part of which is here introduced, simply because it serves to illustrate the language *every family*, πᾶσα πατριά, in Eph., iii., 15. "And what (means) all faces are turned into paleness? Rabbi Johanan says, *the family which is above and the family which is below* (פמליא של מעלה ופמליא של מטה), in the time when the holy one, blessed be he, will say, these are the work of my hands, and these are the work of my hands: how shall I destroy the one before the other?" The Jewish comment, printed in the margin, explains, "the family which is above and the family which is below," of "the angels and Israel." The Talmudical writer proceeds as follows: "Rab says Israel are about *to eat the years* of the Messiah. Says Rabbi Joseph, true, but who *eats of him?* Do Hillek and Billek *eat of*

THE DISCOURSE. 87

him?* in opposition to the words of Hillel, who said, there is no Messiah for Israel, for a long time ago *they ate him*, in the days of Hezekiah. Says Rav, he did not create the world except for David; and Samuel says, for Moses; and Rabbi Johanan says, for Messiah. What is his name? They of the house of Rabbi Shiloh say, that Shiloh is his name, as it is said, until Shiloh come.—Gen., xlix., 10. They of the house of Yenoi say, that Yenon is his name, as it is said, his name shall live forever, with the sun his name shall be perpetuated (ינון, yenon, Ps. lxxii., 17). He who is of the house of Rabbi Chaninah says, Chaninah is his name, as it is said, because he will not show you mercy (חנינה, chaninah, Jer., xvi., 13). And some say that Menachem, the son of Hezekiah, is his name, as it is said, for the comforter (מנחם, menachem) who should restore my soul is far from me —Lam., i., 16. And our Rabbis say, leprous of the house of the Rabbi is his name, as it is said, but he bore our sickness, and our sorrows he sustained them, and we regarded him smitten (נגוע, the original for smitten, is sometimes used of leprosy), stricken by God and afflicted."—Isa., liii., 4. BABYLONIAN TALMUD, treatise SANHEDRIM, fol. 98, 2, towards the bottom. Then, after a very preposterous application of several other texts to the Messiah, the writer remarks: " Rabbi Hillel says,

* Hillek and Billek are the names of certain judges in Sodom, according to Rabbi SOLOMON JARCHI, followed by LIGHTFOOT, Works, vol. ii., p. 554, fol., London, 1684. BUXTORF considers them as fictitious persons.—Lex. Talmud., p. 777.

not for them, for Israel is Messiah, for a long time ago *they ate him*, in the days of Hezekiah." He proceeds, then, to introduce Rabbi Joseph, refuting Hillel by saying, that Hezekiah died under the first temple, and that under the second Zechariah prophesies of the Messiah, and says, " Rejoice greatly, O daughter of Zion, shout, O daughter of Jerusalem, behold, thy king cometh unto thee," &c. (ix., 9).

Now let us examine Dr. Wiseman's criticism on the words of Hillel, as explained by some Protestant divines. " These words," says he, " Lightfoot quotes in a tone of triumph. ' Behold, *eating the Messiah*, and yet no complaints upon the phraseology. Hillel is, indeed, blamed for saying that the Messiah was so eaten that he will no longer be for Israel; but on the form of speech not the slightest scruple is expressed. For they clearly understood what was meant by the *eating of the Messiah;* that is, that in the days of Ezechias they became partakers of the Messiah, received him with avidity, embraced him joyfully, and, as it were, absorbed him; whence he was not to be expected at any future period." '* The author's first remark, that "the phrase of Hillel is so obscure as to be unintelligible," contains an admission of what is certainly very true, namely, that he did not understand it. But, with singular

* The author refers to Lightfoot's Horæ Hebraicæ, Oper., tom. ii., Rotterdam, 1686, p. 626. In the London edition of his works in English, 1684, the passage occurs with some unimportant difference in the language in vol. ii., p. 554.

inconsistency, he immediately tells us that the meaning is, " Messiah was destroyed or consumed in the days of Ezechiah," thus giving a very clear sense to what he had just said is so dark "that it cannot be understood." His next remark, that Lightfoot's meaning cannot be the true one, because " it would be absurd to reason that the Messiah, promised solemnly by God, was to be withheld because persons loved, embraced, and absorbed him spiritually before his coming," is sufficiently answered by a single line from that author himself, which occurs immediately after the quotation just made from him. "Gloss upon the place. *Messiah will come no more to Israel, for Hezekiah was the Messiah.*"*

The cardinal proceeds: "The Jewish doctors themselves did not understand the words of Hillel in Lightfoot's sense. These are the words of the Talmud: ' Rab said, Israel will *eat the years* of the Messiah. (The gloss explains this by "the abundance of *the times* of the Messiah will belong to Israel!") Rab Joseph said truly, but who will eat of it? (*the abundance*). Will Chillek and Billck eat of it? This was said to meet the saying of Hillel,' &c.

" The Rabbins, therefore, understood the words of this doctor, not as applying to the Messiah, but to the *abundance of his times ;* and then the figure

* It is hardly necessary to remind the reader that the absurdity of some notions of the Rabbis does not affect their relevancy to philological inquiries.

H 2

is not in the *eating*, but in the word *Messiah*. Did they understand him rightly? Then Lightfoot's interpretation is totally wrong, and no parallelism exists between these words and those of our Saviour; for he certainly did not mean to inculcate the necessity of eating the abundance of his times. Did they misunderstand Hillel, and was it only Dr. Lightfoot who first arrived at his meaning? Then it follows that Hillel, in these phrases, departed from the intelligible use of language, and consequently ceases to be a criterion for explaining it."

The reader cannot fail to observe, that Dr. Wiseman's exposition relates to one only of the places alleged from the Talmud. The saying of Hillel, which is twice stated in the quotation as above given, still remains to be explained: "Not for Israel is Messiah, for a long time ago *they ate him* in the days of Hezekiah." It is also to be noted, that he introduces the gloss on the Talmud in immediate connexion with the text of it. Lightfoot does the same thing, merely to give in passing the Jewish comment. But our learned author, not content with this legitimate use of the gloss, adapts the words of it to his own purpose, as if they were a continuous portion of the Talmudical text. The pronoun IT, by which he translates the original suffixes והו and ה, is printed in capitals, and made to relate to its supposed antecedent *abundance*. The author could hardly have failed to perceive, that the singular pronoun could not refer to a plural antecedent *years*, and therefore he introduces the gloss, in which the word *abundance* occurs, and translates the suffix by the word *it*, although it can refer to no other word than Messiah, which immediately precedes it, and ought to be rendered *him*. And farther, what must the reader think when he is informed that this supposed antecedent is no part of the Talmud, but occurs in a Jewish commentary written hundreds of years after the sayings of Rab and Rabbi Hillel had been published in that body of Hebrew law! The gloss on this most ancient work was written by RABBI SOLOMON JARCHI, commonly called RASHE, who flourished in the eleventh century. What would be thought of an expositor of Homer who should find an antecedent to one of the great poet's pronouns in the gloss of his commentator Eustathius? and particularly when the antecedent had been just before expressed by the bard himself? The only apology for Dr. Wiseman is, that he does not understand what he has undertaken to explain; and notwithstanding his confident censure of Dr. Lightfoot, to whom he seems to be indebted for what he does know on this point of Rabbinical learning, he might profitably sit at the feet of that great master of Israelitish literature.*

* The high authority of Lightfoot is conceded by Dr. Wiseman, accompanied by a remark which will suggest to the reader a well-known proverb: "Let Dr. Turton listen to a commentator of his own Church, compared to whom all its modern ones are pigmies." This introduces a quotation from Lightfoot's Horæ, Reply, &c., p. 177.

But we must not yet part with Rashe's gloss. It contains satisfactory evidence that the interpretation which our author dismisses in such a summary way is the only true one; for it explains the clause, "Israel are about to eat the years of the Messiah," by the language, "the abundance which shall be in those days shall be for Israel," which evidently denotes enjoyment and satiety, and not "destruction." And this is farther evident from what he afterward remarks on the words of Hillel. "Not Messiah for Israel: because Hezekiah was Messiah, and of him are said all the prophecies; (as), I will cause the horn of the house of Israel to bud; and he shall stand and feed in the strength of the Lord."* The reader may now judge whether Dr. Lightfoot, and other eminent divines learned in Rabbinical lore, who have explained the words of the Talmud the same way with himself, are less entitled to consideration in a question of this sort than Dr. Wiseman.

Since now the Jews were accustomed to the use of such figures in order to express a reception of truth in the mind and heart, and since it is admitted that the figure, as employed in the former portion of our Lord's discourse, was so understood by them, what should have hindered them from applying the same figure, amplified and fully developed, to the same great truth? Certainly, as Paulus says, "the discourse of Jesus would not have been unintelligible to the Jews, if they had wished

* Ezek., xxix., 31. Mic., v., 4.

to understand him."* We are compelled, however reluctantly, to apply his own language on another occasion: "Why do ye not understand my speech? because *ye cannot hear* my word."† Your ignorance, prejudice, passion, whole internal character, form the great insurmountable barrier, which prevents your seeing and embracing the truth.

It will most probably be urged, that the figure of eating and drinking does not fully come up to the strong expressions, "eat the flesh and drink the blood." And it is certainly true, as Tittmann has remarked, that not a single example of such a use of these phrases can be alleged, and that the forms of expression are peculiar to our Lord alone.‡ It is true, also, as he moreover says, that "the Jews could not at that time have understood the force of the language;" but not for the reason which Wiseman's representation of this writer would naturally suggest, because "the sense put on the words by Protestants is contrary to usage;" but because "the preconceived opinions which had taken possession of their minds obliged our Lord to avoid the use of *proper*§ and perspicuous terms, and to express himself in *tropical* diction."‖ But he goes on to observe (what has already

---

* Commentar über das Evangelium des Johannes, Leipsic, 1812, p. 355.   † John, viii., 43.   ‡ See Wiseman, page 87.

§ He employs the word *propriis* in a technical sense, in contradistinction to *figurative*.

‖ Tittmanni Meletemata Sacra sive Commentarius in Evangelium Johannis, Lips., 1816, p. 272

been stated in this Essay), that "the Jews themselves gave occasion to the language," and that "throughout the place is figurative."* The Saviour does but take up and draw out the objector's language; the germ of the expressions is contained in the preceding part of the discourse. The rule laid down by Dr. Wiseman, that, in conducting philological investigations, we must "study words as they are used in peculiar circumstances," a rule which is founded in common sense, and applied in the daily intercourse of men, satisfactorily accounts for the use of the terms. As I have already stated and illustrated this judicious principle, it is sufficient, in this connexion, simply to recall it to the reader's attention.

Should it, after all, be objected, that if we suppose such a faith as has been described to be what is meant, the language is obscure, and the sentiment not conveyed with that clearness which might ordinarily be expected; it may be replied with force, and agreeably to Scripture analogy, that to such hearers our Lord was in no respects bound to convey his doctrines in the clearest and most intelligible terms. They were not men of honest and simple minds, disposed to receive the Gospel, but captious opponents of the truth, in whom the understanding was darkened by the perversion and prejudice of the heart. It is a serious consideration, which ought to be deeply impressed

* Pages 275, 276.

on the mind of every one who proposes to search after religious truth, that the arrangement of divine Providence makes the acquisition dependant, in no slight degree, on the moral character of the seeker. The humble, docile, candid, and diligent inquirer is the one most likely to be successful; while the conceited and prejudiced, who does not feel an interest in the subject strong enough to impel him to careful and habitual attention, is allowed to persist in that very ignorance which, by a fatuity not at all uncommon, he mistakes for a more than ordinary degree of wisdom. It is as much the appointment of God as it is the decision of Christ, that "if any man will do his will, he shall know whether the doctrine be of God"* or man. And in harmony with the same fundamental axiom, divine wisdom declares, that "the words of her mouth are all plain to him that understandeth," that is, who sincerely loves the truth, and properly attends to instruction.†

From what has been said, I conclude that this part of our Lord's discourse, like the preceding, urges the necessity of a living faith in Christ, acting on the atonement which he was about to offer, and expresses the union with himself which such a faith produces, and the blessed consequences resulting. While the words fitly denote the action of such faith on its divine object during the

* John, vii., 17.
† Prov., viii., 8, 9. This is implied in the word מֵבִין, and is given by the Chaldee and Syriac versions.

various occasions of a religious life, they are particularly appropriate to that action in the Sacrament of the Lord's Supper, which our Church, in the spirit of Scripture and the language of antiquity, most properly enjoins on the communicant in the terms: "*Feed on him in thy heart by* FAITH." In the same truly Christian spirit does she comfort the dying believer, who is prevented by uncontrollable circumstances from commemorating his Master's death in the eucharist, by assuring him "that, if he do truly repent him of his sins, and steadfastly believe that Jesus Christ hath suffered death upon the cross for him, and shed his blood for his redemption, earnestly remembering the benefits he hath thereby, and giving him hearty thanks therefor, *he doth eat and drink the body and blood* of our Saviour Christ profitably to his soul's health, although he do not receive the sacrament with his mouth."* In the words of St. Augustin, "*Believe, and thou hast eaten.*"†

The remainder of the chapter does not require very particular examination. It relates the fact, which need not be surprising to any, that the doctrine was objected to as harsh, and became an occasion of the apostacy of many who had before professed attachment to the teacher, while the true disciples persevered in their faith and love, verses 60, 61, 66–71. It contains, also, our Lord's own correction of the erroneous and literal sense

---

* Third Rubric in the Office for the Communion of the Sick.
† In Johan. Evang., cap. 6, Tract. xxv., § 12, tom. ii., par. ii., p. 354

of his words, verses 62, 63, and his reference to the leading cause of the error, want of faith produced by the Father's influence, verses 64, 65. I shall conclude this part of the discussion by examining the great Master's correction.

"Does this offend you?" throw an obstacle in the way of your faith and perseverance, and incline you to reject my doctrine? " If, then, you should see the Son of Man ascending where he was before?" These words may be intended to convey the thought, that the harshness of his supposed meaning would necessarily be increased after his ascension, when his flesh and blood should be removed, and his bodily presence no more be continued; and thus they would amplify the supposed ground of stumbling. As if he had said : " If this doctrine is now so distasteful to you, how abhorrent to your feelings and partial reasonings will it appear after I shall have resumed my former condition in heaven !" According to this view, the verse, instead of containing anything like a solution of the difficulty, only draws it out with the more particularity. The solution, if there be one, begins with the next words. If, however, the verse be regarded as the commencement of the solution, it unquestionably implies this most important point, namely, that the literal exposition is a palpable absurdity and contradiction, which a sane mind, not under some undue extraneous influence, could hardly be thought capable of entertaining. Then it will be as if Christ had said :

"Does my language present an impediment to your faith? You have grossly misunderstood me; and my ascension to heaven will prove to you that the literal sense in which you have taken my words cannot possibly be the true one." Whichever of these views may be thought preferable, the meaning of the next verse will not be materially affected. "It is the Spirit that quickeneth, the flesh profiteth nothing; the words that I speak unto you are spirit and are life." It is necessary to give the general sense of these words.

If the literal meaning be adhered to, "the flesh" must be explained of Christ's body, and then the assertion will be, that his body, even if it were to be eaten and incorporated with the substance of the recipient, would not benefit him. Neither Scripture nor reason affords any ground for denying the truth of this assertion. And this sense is given to the word *flesh* in this verse by several distinguished divines. Thus CRANMER, for example, after quoting our Saviour's language, remarks: "These words our Saviour Christ spake, to lift up their minds from earth to heaven, and from carnal to spiritual eating, that they should not phantasy that they should with their teeth eat him present here on earth; for his flesh, so eaten, saith he, should nothing profit them. And yet so they should not eat him; for he would take his body away from them and ascend with it into heaven, and then by faith, and not with teeth, they should spiritually eat him, sitting at the right hand of the

Father. And, therefore, saith he, the words which I do speak be spirit and life; that is to say, are not to be understood that we shall eat Christ with our teeth grossly and carnally, but that we shall spiritually and ghostly with our faith eat him, being carnally absent from us in heaven, and in such wise as Abraham and other holy fathers did eat him many years before he was incarnated and born."* FABER, who cites the passage, agrees with the archbishop. " When we take in the entire context of the whole discourse, which teaches us both that no man can be saved *without* eating Christ's flesh and drinking his blood, and that every man who *does* thus eat and who *does* thus drink will infallibly obtain eternal salvation; and when we farther note the necessary tenour of the argument from the Lord's previous descent to his then future ascent, I really think that words can scarcely be plainer than those wherein Christ avowedly contrasts the spirit of his discourse with the letter. My flesh, we may view him as saying, if it were possible for the infinite millions of mankind all grossly to eat of it, would, under *that* aspect, profit them nothing to eternal salvation. The whole context of the discourse shows, that by the *flesh* we must understand our Lord's own flesh which he had declared he would give his people to eat; and by the *spirit*, a spiritual manducation as op-

* Defence of the True and Catholic Doctrine of the Sacrament, &c. Remains of THOMAS CRANMER, D.D., Oxford, 1833, vol. ii., p. 378.

posed to a gross carnal manducation. Under this aspect, the following will be the sense of the passage: The flesh of which I speak, namely, my own material flesh, would profit you nothing in the way of obtaining everlasting life, even were it possible for you to eat it bodily with your teeth when I shall have ascended up to heaven."* HAMMOND seems to have taken the same view, and WHITBY explains the term of the body of Christ.

Still, a figurative meaning of the word, in this place, may consistently be maintained, on account of the antithesis with spirit, and the ordinary usage of Scripture in such cases. The term *flesh* is so often employed in a tropical sense, that figure of some sort may well be admitted in this instance, although it is not easy to say very definitely within what limits, and by what literal expressions, the thought is to be confined. The terms *flesh* and *carnal* are used, and most naturally, for the external, in contradistinction to the inward, and hence to designate man as what he appears to be: as, "All *flesh* is grass; the Word was made *flesh*;"† for the merely outward, superficial, imperfect, in which sense they are applied to the rites of the law, as when St. Paul asks the Galatians, "Are ye so foolish? having begun in the spirit, are ye now made perfect by the *flesh?*" and speaks of Christ as a priest, "not after the power

* Christ's Discourse at Capernaum, &c., chap. iv., p. 92, 93, 95. London, 1840.
† Isa., xl., 5. John, i., 14.

of a *carnal* commandment," and of the legal services as "*carnal* ordinances;"* for what either is, or is considered as inadequate, low, and comparatively contemptible, as where it is said, "If we have sown unto you spiritual things, is it a great thing if we shall reap your *carnal* things?" And again: "The weapons of our warfare are not *carnal*, but mighty," &c. ;† and, lastly, for what is vile, corrupt, sinful, as in the texts, "I am *carnal*, sold under sin;" "Who walk not after the *flesh*, but after the spirit," and others to the same effect.‡ And, on the other hand, the words spirit and spiritual are often employed to denote the inward, excellent, perfect, holy, and divine. This is evident from the following passages: "What man knoweth the things of a man save the *spirit* of a man which is in him?" They "did all eat the same *spiritual* meat, and drink the same *spiritual* drink." "He that was born after the flesh persecuted him that was born after the *spirit*."§ To this view of the usage of Scripture it may be added, that the previous use of the word flesh would naturally have led our Lord to adopt it in a modified sense; as is the case with other words elsewhere. Of this we have instances in St. Paul's writings. Thus, he employs the word *sleep* in different modifications of meaning even in the

* Gal., iii., 3. Heb., vii., 16; ix., 10.
† 1 Cor., ix., 11; 2 Cor., x., 4.
‡ Rom., vii., 14; viii., 4-9. John, iii., 6.
§ 1 Cor., ii., 11; x., 3, 4. Gal., iv., 29. To these might be added 1 Cor., xv., 45. Rom., i., 4. John, iv., 24.

same connexion, and also *present* and *absent*. And in the epistle to the Hebrews, the word *camp* is used in a figurative sense, although it had just before been employed in its literal meaning.* In accordance, therefore, with these facts, and in perfect harmony with the common meaning of these terms, flesh and spirit, is the view which expounds the verse thus: 'That apprehension of my language which is limited to the outward and superficial, which accords with the secular and degrading, which is compatible with the vile and sinful, the corrupt and corrupting naturalness of the heart, is not only useless, but positively injurious.† The deeper meaning brings happiness and joy. The 'more excellent way' which it opens, the practical, soul-stirring principle which it develops, the heavenly and divine life which, when rightly received, it causes to germinate and flourish—these constitute its vitality and real worth.' It is unnecessary to say that this closing declaration of our Lord is in most perfect keeping with the view given of his discourse in the preceding analysis.

* 1 Thess., v., 6, 7, 10. 2 Cor., v., 6, 8, 9. Heb., xiii., 13, 11.

† This verbal addition is implied, though not expressed, and is in accordance with numerous other instances in Scripture where less is said than is evidently intended. Illustration seems unnecessary; yet the reader is referred to Matt., xii., 20, and to Rom., i., 16, compared with Gal., vi., 14.

PART III.
VIEW OF THE EARLY FATHERS AND OF SOME MODERN DIVINES.

I PROCEED now to present to the reader's attention some quotations from the more prominent of the early fathers, in reference to the view entertained by them of the nature and design of our Lord's discourse. Lest he should find these less clear and luminous than he may have expected such a representation to be, it may not be amiss to remind him that most of these good men were chiefly interested in spreading a knowledge of the Gospel, and in cultivating its practical influence on their own characters. Formal and critical interpretation will be looked for in vain in the writers of the first three centuries. Their expositions of Scripture must be sought in various treatises on topics of philosophy and theology, in defences of the Christian faith, in epistolary writings, and in works composed in opposition to prevalent errors. Commentary, in the later sense of the word, was hardly known. Modern theologians have differed in their views of the exposition given by these fathers of the chapter under consideration; some contending that they understood it directly of the eucharist, while others maintain that they only apply part of its language to this sacrament. This fact is itself sufficient evidence that the exposition of these fathers is not so definite and perspicuous as some persons, unacquainted with their works, may suppose. Mr. JOHNSON maintains that they interpret it primarily and properly of the eucharist, and only remotely of receiving Christ's doctrine or precepts. "I conceive that the fathers never doubted but that this mystical or spiritual sense was that which our Saviour primarily intended." He uses the words "mystical" and "spiritual" in the sense of *original*, and in contradistinction to *applicable:* "Besides the primary and direct sense of the text, the ancients commonly supposed that there was a reductive or anagogical meaning in which it might be taken." "They might be fully persuaded that John, vi., was first and most properly to be understood of the eucharist; and yet, at the same time, be of opinion that it might likewise, in a more remote way, be applied to receiving of Christ's doctrine or precepts. And, so far as I am able to penetrate into the judgment of the ancients in this particular, I can see no reason to believe that they did ever understand John, vi., of believing Christ's doctrine or receiving his word by faith, *extra cœnam*, to be meant by our Saviour otherwise than in this anagogical way of interpretation."* On the other hand, Dr. WATERLAND advocates

---

* The Unbloody Sacrifice and Altar, unveiled and supported. By JOHN JOHNSON, M.A., Vicar of Cranbrook, London, 1724 part i., chap. ii., sec. v., p. 358, 359.

the opinion that the early fathers do not interpret this chapter directly of the eucharist, but only apply it to that sacrament. "They who judge that the fathers in general, or almost universally, do interpret John, vi., of the eucharist, appear not to distinguish between *interpreting* and *applying*. It was right to *apply* the *general* doctrine of John, vi., to the particular case of the eucharist considered as worthily received; because the spiritual feeding there mentioned is the thing signified in the eucharist, yea, and performed likewise. After we have sufficiently proved from other Scriptures that in and by the eucharist ordinarily such spiritual food is conveyed, it is then right to *apply* all that our Lord, by St. John, says in the *general* to that *particular* case. And this, indeed, the fathers commonly did. But such *application* does not amount to *interpreting* that chapter of the eucharist. For example, the words, 'except ye eat the flesh of Christ, &c., you have no life in you,' do not mean directly, that you have no life without the eucharist, but that you have no life without participating in our Lord's passion. Nevertheless, since the eucharist is one way of participating of the passion, and a very considerable one, it was very pertinent and proper to urge the doctrine of that chapter, both for the clearer understanding the beneficial nature of the eucharist, and for the exciting Christians to a frequent and devout reception of it. Such was the use which some early fathers made of John, vi., as our Church also does at this day, and that very justly, though I will not say that some of the later fathers did not extend it farther."*

I have particularly mentioned these two learned divines, because, although both are distinguished by profound and extensive acquaintance with ancient writers, they cannot agree in determining the sense which the early fathers intended to give of this chapter. And this fact is sufficient to show that the obscurity in the inspired page itself is not always removed by the expositions even of the best of these writers. The interpretation may chance to be no clearer than the text, and equally to require philological investigation and antiquarian research. The view of Dr. Waterland does appear to me the most probable. Although, after the fourth century, the discourse was often explained directly in reference to the eucharist; and so much were the fathers generally in the habit of associating in their minds the thing signified with its sign, or, to approach nearer to their own language, the substance with the sacrament, that, in explaining the discourse of spiritual eating and drinking, several of them connect with it a refer-

---

* A Review of the Doctrine of the Eucharist, as laid down in Scripture and Antiquity. By DANIEL WATERLAND, D.D., Cambridge, 1737, chap. vi., p. 149, 150. Or the seventh volume of his works, published at Oxford in 1823. The reader who undertakes to peruse Mr. Johnson's work would do well to read and meditate on the brief but masterly notice of it in Waterland's appendix to a charge, entitled, "The Christian Sacrifice explained," in the eighth volume of his works, p. 180–223.

ence to sacramental. That some of the fathers either are not or do not appear to be always consistent with themselves in explaining parts of this discourse, is attributed by LAMPE to the fact, that in the sacrament of the eucharist they admitted not an oral, but a spiritual manducation, by faith, of Christ's body and blood.*

I submit the following quotations from the early fathers, with such comment merely as seems necessary. They are the most important passages bearing on our Lord's discourse which their works contain. I have endeavoured to give their true meaning, but the accompanying originals will enable the competent reader to form his own judgment. To have quoted everything on the subject in these writings, adding such remarks as a critical investigation of their purport and application might require, would have swelled this Essay into a large volume, without in any great degree increasing its usefulness.

IGNATIUS is the earliest writer who seems to allude to this chapter of St. John. In his epistle to the Romans, after speaking of his desire to die, and of a living principle within him, "which says, come to the Father," he remarks, "I delight not in corruptible food, nor in the pleasures of this life; I wish for the bread of God, which is the flesh of Jesus Christ of the race of David, and the

* Hæc inconstantia Patrum proculdubio inde orta est, quod in Sacramento Eucharistiæ non oralem, sed spiritualem fidei manducationem admitterent. Commentarius Evang. secundum Johannem, Amst., 1727, 4to, tom. ii., p. 257.

drink I wish for is his blood, which is incorruptible love. No longer do I wish to live according to men."*

It is particularly worthy of notice, that the author does not formally quote any text, but merely alludes to the 33d, 51st, and 55th verses, as if the general subject of the discourse were in his mind. This peculiarity characterizes the quotations and references to Scripture in the smaller epistles of Ignatius, while the larger generally contain the texts full and accurate; a fact which goes far to settle the authority of the one, as it harmonizes with the condition and circumstances of the writer, and also to show that the others are the production of a later age, and were written under different circumstances.

Mr. Johnson gives another exposition of the words rendered "incorruptible love," by adding to this evidently correct translation the clause, "or an incorruptible love feast!" And he endeavours to show that the holy martyr, harassed by the fatigues of his journey, and by the confinement to which he was subjected by his guards, his "leopards," as he elsewhere calls them, here expresses his wish to partake of the Lord's Supper! "I own he was just before speaking of going to the Father, and in the following words he

* 'Οὐχ ἥδομαι τροφῇ φθορᾶς, οὐδὲ ἡδοναῖς τοῦ βίου τούτου· ἄρτον τοῦ θεοῦ θέλω, ὅ ἐστι σάρξ Ἰησοῦ Χριστοῦ τοῦ ἐκ γένους Δαβίδ· καὶ πόμα θέλω τὸ αἷμα αὐτοῦ, ὅ ἐστιν ἀγάπη ἄφθαρτος.—Epist. to the Romans, chap. vii.

declares that he desires not human life; but I cannot think it any incoherence, when he was speaking of going to the Father and not desiring to live here, to express his holy hunger and thirst after that which has always been thought the most proper viaticum, the Holy Eucharist. 'Tis probable he had not been permitted, while under the custody of his inhuman keepers, in his voyage, to celebrate the eucharist, or that he durst not do it for fear of having the mysteries profaned by them; but he hoped when he came to Rome to have an opportunity of refreshing himself with that divine repast; and I suppose he expresses these hopes and desires in the words now cited. And I am pretty sure that there is no incongruity in this supposition; whereas eating of Christ's flesh in another world is a way of expression somewhat unaccountable."* To endeavour to disprove such a supposition appears to me wholly unnecessary. It is evident that Ignatius alludes to our Lord's discourse at Capernaum; and it is equally evident from his language itself, from the connexion in which it stands, and from the circumstances under which the epistle was written, that the holy man has in mind, not a participation of the eucharist, but a spiritual enjoyment of Christ, and that principally after his martyrdom. This is to me the undoubted meaning of the spiritually-minded bishop, and, to employ the language of Mr. Johnson, " St. Ignatius, after all.

* Unbloody Sacrifice, part i., chap. ii., sec. v., p. 394.

is instead of a thousand witnesses."* "To me," says Dr. Waterland, "it appears a clear point that he thought not of communicating, but of dying. I see no impropriety in his feeding on the flesh and blood of Christ in a state of glory. Our enjoyment in a world to come is entirely founded in the merits of Christ's passion, and our Lord's intercession for us stands on the same bottom. Our spiritual food, both above and below, is the enjoyment of the same Christ, the Lamb slain. The future feast upon the fruits of his atonement is but the continuation and completion of the present."†

The phrase " bread of God," which occurs in this passage, is employed also by Ignatius in his epistle to the Ephesians. " Let no one deceive himself. Unless any one be within the altar, he is deprived of the bread of God."‡ It is assumed by Johnson as undeniable that he uses it of the Lord's Supper. " By calling the eucharist the bread of God he clearly refers to John, vi., 33 ;" " it is certain that by that phrase he means the eucharist."§ But so far is this from being certain, that it does not appear to be even probable. The language is used in the same sense in which it is employed in the verse referred to, that is to say, of Christ himself, who came from God to be the author and sustainer of our spiritual life. This

* Unbloody Sacrifice, part i., chap. ii., sec. v., p. 392.
† P. 153, 154.
‡ Μηδεὶς πλανάσθω · ἐὰν μή τις ᾖ ἐιτὺς τοῦ θυσιαστηριυν, ὑστεοεῖται τοῦ ἄρτου τοῦ θεοῦ.—Chap. v. § P. 346, 394.

alone would be sufficient reason for applying to him such figurative language; but inasmuch as the phrase is frequently used of sacrifices under the law,* it doubtless is chosen with the intention of representing him as also the great sacrifice whereby alone God is propitiated. In John, vi., 33, our Saviour calls himself, and afterward Ignatius calls him, " the bread of God, as he was a sacrifice for the sins of the world, and mysteriously to be eaten as such."† This is almost self-evident as regards the first passage in Ignatius. In the other the word " altar" will doubtless be thought by many to favour Johnson's opinion. But it is a mistake to suppose that Ignatius intends by this word to designate the Lord's Table. That author understands it of the " altar-room," by being called up into which, and there " eating the sacrifice," he says, that " Christian people are dignified beyond the old peculium" (the Jews), and " within which all communicants did unquestionably, in St. Ignatius's time, go, in order to receive the eucharist," although afterward " they were prohibited from entering into the altar-room."‡ He avoids the absurdity of the literal meaning of persons being within an altar, by giving a sense to the word which is wholly unfounded, and by adhering to a literal meaning of the whole clause, alike unworthy of the martyr and his subject, and

* Levit., xxi., 6, 8, 17, 22; xxii., 25.
† I willingly adopt the language of the learned writer referred to. See Unbloody Sacrifice, part i., p. 425.
‡ Unbloody Sacrifice, p. 347.

inconsistent with the peculiar circumstances under which he wrote. There is hardly any reason to doubt that here, and in the three other places in which the term occurs, Ignatius uses the word in a figurative sense, for the Church, or for Christ himself, in connexion with whom, as around an altar or in a temple, all spiritual blessings do, as it were, cluster. That, in the place just cited, he means the Church, is evident from the preceding context, and from that which immediately follows. The whole passage runs thus: "How must I esteem you happy who are so intimately united with him (the bishop), as the Church is with Jesus Christ and Jesus Christ with the Father, that all things may accord in unity! Let no one deceive himself. Unless any one be within the altar, he is deprived of the bread of God. For if the prayer of one and two have so great efficacy, how much rather will that of the bishop and the whole Church!" To the Magnesians he says: "There is one Lord Jesus Christ, than whom nothing is more excellent. Run together, therefore, all as to one temple, as to one altar, as to one Jesus Christ" (chap. vii.). To the Trallians: "He that is within the altar is pure" (chap. vii). In both these places the meaning is also plain. In the only remaining one in which the term occurs, in the epistle to the Philadelphians, it might be understood of the Lord's Table, and has often been so explained. See Suicer's Thesaurus, under θυσιαστήριον, ii., 1, d; Parkhurst's Greek Lexicon, No. II., and THOLUCK on Heb., xiii., 10. The words are these: " There is one flesh of our Lord Jesus Christ, and one cup for unity in his blood, one altar" (chap. iv.). Still I cannot but think that a careful attention to the context, and particularly the immediately preceding chapter, will satisfy the reader that the meaning already suggested is preferable. The apostolic man is urging those to whom he writes to unity, and the term *altar* may with as much propriety be understood of the Church as of the Lord's Table; and the probability that such is its meaning here is strengthened by the fact that such is the undoubted sense of it elsewhere. The context is as follows: " As many as shall repent and come to the unity of the Church, these shall be God's, that they may live according to Jesus Christ. Be not deceived, my brethren. If any one follow a schismatic, he shall not inherit the kingdom of God. If any one walk after a different opinion, he is not in harmony with Christ's passion. Be careful, therefore, to use one eucharist; for there is one flesh of our Lord Jesus Christ, and one cup for unity in his blood, one altar." It is very surprising that any one should wish to give to these places a meaning which refers chiefly to what is material or local.*

* I may take this opportunity of remarking, that the best of the Greek fathers give a similar figurative meaning to the word altar in Heb., xiii., 10. Thus, THEODORET, on that epistle: "This," says he, " is much more precious than the old, for that was a shadow of

I do not find anything in JUSTIN MARTYR bearing on the interpretation of this chapter, and therefore pass on to IRENÆUS. There is only one passage within my knowledge in the works of this father which may be thought to allude to this chapter, and even this is of doubtful application. He says that our Lord did not come to us, as he might have done, in his incorruptible glory, which we could not have borne; but "the perfect bread of the Father supplied us, as babes with milk, himself, which was his advent according to man, that we, nourished by the breast, as it were, of his flesh, and accustomed by such lactation to eat and drink the Word of God, might be able to retain in ourselves the bread of immortality, which

this. That receives the irrational sacrifices, but this that which is rational and divine."—Opera, tom. iii., p. 460. And CHRYSOSTOM, Hom. xi., on Heb. (chap. vi.): "For see, we have above the victim, above the priest, above the sacrifice. Let us, therefore, offer such sacrifices as can be offered on such an altar. No more sheep and oxen; no more blood and odour of burned fat. All these are abolished, and in their place is substituted a rational worship."—Opera, tom. xiii., Bened. edit., p. 114. He then proceeds to describe this worship as spiritual, consisting in modesty, temperance, almsgiving, and other virtues. Also, CYRILL of Alexandria: "He, therefore, is the altar, and he the incense and high-priest."—On Adoration, lib. ix., p 310; as quoted in Suicer, ubi sup., ii., 1, a. THEOPHYLACT probably understood it of the Lord's Table: "After remarking on the 9th verse, that meats are not to be regarded, he says" (that is, the author of the epistle) "that we also have what should be regarded, not, indeed, in such meats, but in the altar of the unbloody sacrifice of the quickening body."—Opera, vol. ii., p. 758. Cyrill's language appears to me to contain the fullest meaning. As if the Apostle had said, all the blessings of the Gospel meet in Christ. To speak of the altar, is to speak of the sacrifice, of the priest, of the temple, and of all connected with and flowing from them.

is the spirit of the Father."* If the Bishop of Lyons does refer to John, vi., he evidently does not consider the discourse as relating directly to the eucharist, as he is discoursing of Christ's incarnation, by which the eating and drinking which he speaks of are effected. A spiritual union and incorporation with the Word is certainly intended.

TERTULLIAN comments on some passages in this chapter, if not in the most perspicuous manner, yet clearly enough to show that he had no idea of explaining it directly of the eucharist. He is proving that our Lord's expression, "the flesh profiteth nothing," does not militate against the doctrine of the resurrection. "Although he says the flesh profiteth nothing, the meaning must be drawn from the subject of the declaration. For, because they considered his discourse as harsh and intolerable, as if he had decided that his own flesh was to be truly eaten by them, in order that he might arrange the state of salvation in (reference to) the Spirit, he premised, it is the Spirit that quickeneth. And consequently he subjoined, the flesh profiteth nothing, that is, in quickening. This is followed, also, by what he intends us to understand by spirit: the words which I have

* Διὰ τοῦτο, ὡς νηπίοις, ὁ ἄρτος ὁ τέλειος τοῦ Πατρὸς γάλα ἡμῖν ἑαυτὸν παρέσχεν, ὅπερ ἦν ἡ κατ' ἄνθρωπον αὐτοῦ παρουσία, ἵνα ὡς ὑπὸ μασθοῦ τῆς σαρκὸς αὐτοῦ τραφέντες, καὶ διὰ τῆς τοιαύτης γαλακτουργίας ἐθισθέντες τρώγειν καὶ πίνειν τὸν λόγον τοῦ θεοῦ, τὸν τῆς ἀθανασίας ἄρτον, ὅπερ ἐστὶ τὸ πνεῦμα τοῦ Πατρὸς, ἐν ἡμῖν αὐτοῖς κατεσχεῖν δυνηθῶμεν.—Adv. Hær., lib. iv. cap. lxxiv., p. 378, edit. GRABE, Oxon., 1702.

spoken to you are spirit, and they are life. As also before: he that heareth my words and believeth on him that sent me, hath eternal life, and shall not come into judgment, but shall pass from death to life. Constituting, therefore, the Word as the vivifier, because the Word is spirit and life, he called the same also his own flesh, because the Word was made flesh, and is therefore to be earnestly sought for with a view to life, is to be devoured by hearing, ruminated on in the understanding, and digested by faith. For a little before, he had declared his own flesh to be heavenly bread, constantly impressing, by means of the allegory of necessary food, a recollection of their fathers, who had preferred the bread and flesh of the Egyptians to the divine vocation. Adverting, therefore, to their thoughts, because he had perceived that they were scattered, he says, the flesh profiteth nothing. What is there here to destroy the resurrection of the flesh?"*

---

* Etsi carnem ait nihil prodesse, ex materia dicti dirigendus est sensus. Nam, quia durum et intolerabilem existimaverunt sermonem ejus, quasi vere carnem suam illis edendam determinasset; ut in spiritum disponeret statum salutis, præmisit, spiritus est qui vivificat. Atque ita subjunxit, caro nihil prodest; ad vivificandum scilicet. Exequitur etiam quia velit intelligi spiritum, verba quæ locutus sum vobis, spiritus sunt, vita sunt. Sicut et supra; qui audit sermones meos et credit in eum qui me misit, habet vitam eternam, et in judicium non veniet, sed transiet de morte ad vitam. Itaque sermonem constituens vivificatorem, quid spiritus et vita sermo, eundem etiam carnem suam dixit; quia et sermo caro est factus, proinde in causam vitæ appetendus, et devorandus auditu, et ruminandus intellectu, et fide digerendus. Nam et paulo ante, carnem suam panem quoque cœlestem pronunciarat, urgens usquequaque per allegoriam necessa-

Another passage is also worthy of note. "Give us this day our daily bread. This is rather to be understood in a spiritual sense. For Christ is our bread, because Christ is life, and bread is life; I am, says he, the bread of life: and a little before, the bread is the Word of the living God, who came down from heaven. Then, again, because his body is judged* (to be) in the bread; this is my body. Therefore, by praying for daily bread, we pray for perpetuity in Christ, and an indissoluble connexion with his body."†

The application of our Lord's words, "this is my body," in this latter passage, together with others of a similar sort to be found in the writings of the fathers, sufficiently justify the observation which I have already made, that they *apply* to sacramental manducation what they understood to be originally *intended* of spiritual.

CYPRIAN, who reverenced Tertullian as his mas-

---

riorum pabulorum, memoriam patrum, qui panes et carnes Ægyptiorum præverterant divinæ vocationi. Igitur conversus ad cogitatus illorum, quia senserat dispergendos, caro, ait, nihil prodest. Quid hoc ad destruendam carnis resurrectionem ?—Tert., de Resurrectione Carnis, cap. xxxvii., Opera, p. 347, edit. Rigalt, Paris, 1675.

* The original word is censetur, the ambiguity of which I have endeavoured to express by the word *judge*. Johnson does not scruple to render it "*authoritatively declared!*" chap. ii., sec. v., p. 365.

† Panem nostrum quotidianum da nobis hodie, spiritualiter potius intelligamus. Christus enim panis noster est; quia vita Christus, et vita panis. Ego sum, inquit, panis vitæ. Et paulo supra ; panis est sermo Dei vivi, qui descendit de cœlis. Tum quod et corpus ejus in pane censetur, hoc est corpus meum. Itaque, petendo panem quotidianum, perpetuitatem postulamus in Christo et individuitatem a corpore ejus.—De Oratore, cap. vi., p. 131, 132.

ter, affords another illustration of this remark, by applying expressions taken from this chapter to a right participation of Christ in the eucharist. But his language by no means sanctions the conclusion, that he considered the discourse as originally and directly intended of this sacrament. In his treatise on the Lord's Prayer, he comments on the petition, "Give us this day our daily bread," as follows: "This may be understood both spiritually and in its simple meaning; each sense, by the divine blessing, conducing to our welfare. For Christ is the bread of life, and this bread is peculiarly ours. And as we say, our Father, because he is the Father of those who understand and believe, so also we call (him) our bread, because Christ is the bread of us who are intimately conjoined with his body. But we pray that this bread be given to us daily, lest we, who are in Christ and receive the eucharist daily as the food of our salvation, should be separated from Christ's body, inasmuch as, on occasion of some more grievous fault, being debarred from communicating, we are prohibited from the heavenly bread. For he himself proclaims and admonishes, 'I, who came down from heaven, am the bread of life. If any one eat of my bread, he shall live forever. But the bread which I will give is my flesh for the life of the world.' When, therefore, he says, if any one eat of this bread he shall live forever, as it is manifest that those live who belong to his body, and receive the eucharist with a right to communicate; so, on the other hand, it is to be feared and deprecated, lest any one, being debarred, should be separated from Christ's body, should remain at a distance from salvation, he himself employing the threatening language, 'Except ye shall eat the flesh of the Son of Man and shall drink his blood, ye shall have no life in you.'"*

The application of the prayer for daily bread to the eucharist is almost universal with the fathers, and yet it is hardly to be supposed that they understood this as the direct and original purport of the petition as taught by our Lord to his apostles during his lifetime. Being a prayer for sustenance of the whole man, both soul and body, they understood it to comprehend a reference to all the means by which such sustenance might be obtained. And thus Cyprian, in the above quotation, intending to represent Christ himself as spiritually our food, and considering this heavenly sustenance as particularly given in the Lord's supper, directs the attention of his hearers especially to the eucharist.

* "Panem nostrum quotidianum da nobis hodie. Quod potest et spiritaliter et simpliciter intelligi, quia et uterque intellectus utilitate divina proficit ad salutem. Nam panis vitæ Christus est, et panis hic omnium non est, sed noster est. Et quomodo dicimus pater noster, quia intelligentium et credentium pater est; sic et panem nostrum vocamus, quia Christus, noster qui corpus ejus contingimus, panis est. Hunc autem panem dari nobis quotidie postulamus, ne qui in Christo sumus, et eucharistiam quotidie ad cibum salutis accipimus, intercedente aliquo graviore delicto, dum abstenti et non communicantes a cœlesti pane prohibemur, a Christi corpore separemur, ipso prædicante et monente: ego sum panis vitæ qui de cœlo descendi; si quis ederit deo me pane, vivet in æternum; panis autem quem ego

CLEMENT of Alexandria cites several passages from this chapter, and comments on them. After speaking of the difference between milk and meat as figuratively used for spiritual food, with an evident reference to 1 Cor., iii., 2, he proceeds to say: " The Lord in the Gospel according to John hath explained such food by symbols, saying, eat my flesh and drink my blood, expressing, under the allegory of something that might be drunk, the clearness of faith and of the promise, by which the Church, like a man, consisting of many members, is watered and increased, and most closely compacted of both, faith as the body and hope as the soul, as also the Lord, of flesh and blood."*

dedero caro mea est pro sæculi vita. Quando ergo dicit, in æternum vivere si quis ederit de ejus pane, ut manifestum est eos vivere qui corpus ejus attingunt et eucharistiam jure communicationis accipiunt, ita contra timendum est et orandum, ne dum quis abstentus separatur a Christi corpore, procul remaneat a salute; comminante ipso et dicente, nisi ederitis carnem filii hominis et biberitis sanguinem ejus, non habebitis vitam in vobis."—De Oratione Dominica, Opera, Oxon., 1682, p. 146, 147.

* Τὴν τοιάνδε τροφὴν ἀλλάχοθι δὲ ὁ Κύριος, ἐν τῷ κατὰ Ἰωάννην ἐναγγελίῳ, ἑτέρως ἐξήνεγκεν διὰ συμβόλων · φάγεσθε μου τάς σάρκας, εἰπὼν, καὶ πίεσθε μου τὸ αἷμα · ἐναργὲς τῆς πίστεως καὶ τῆς ἐπαγγελίας τὸ πότιμον ἀλληγορῶν, δι' ὧν ἡ ἐκκλησία, καθάπερ ἄνθρωπος, ἐκ πολλῶν συνεστηκυῖα μελῶν, ἄρδεται τε καὶ αὔξεται, συγκροτεῖται τε καὶ συμπήγνυται, ἐξ ἀμφοῖν · σώματος μὲν, τῆς πίστεως, ψυχῆς δε, τῆς ἐλπίδος · ὥσπερ καὶ ὁ Κύριος, ἐκ σαρκὸς καὶ αἵματος.—Pædag., lib. i., cap. vi., p. 100, edit. Sylburg. Lutetiæ (Paris), 1629. The construction and meaning of ἐναργὲς is not clear to me. WATERLAND translates thus: "allegorically signifying the clear liquor of faith and of the promise;" making it qualify τὸ πότιμον, p. 159. FABER renders it adverbially: "he evidently is al-

In the same chapter Clement expresses himself thus: "The Word is all things to the infant, both father and mother, and preceptor and nourisher. Eat, says he, my flesh, and drink my blood. This suitable nutriment for us the Lord supplies. He reaches forth flesh and pours out blood, and nothing is needed for the growth of the infants. O wonderful mystery! He commands us to put off the old and carnal corruption, as also the old nourishment, and to partake of the other new food of Christ; him, if possible, receiving, to lay up within ourselves, and to enclose the Saviour in the breast, in order to render sound the affections of our flesh."* It can hardly be doubted that in

legorizing the drinkableness of faith," &c.—Christ's Discourse at Capernaum fatal to the Doctrine of Transubstantiation, 8vo, p. 113. So also Johnson, p. 360, who introduces it in the midst of a subsequent passage of Clement, and then remarks that the author whose view he is opposing "only produces" a part "of this paragraph!" WHITBY, to whom he probably refers, quotes the passage, but gives no translation of the word: "he allegorically meant the drinking of faith and of the promises."—On v. 53, 54, 7thly. The Bishop of Lincoln, too (Dr. KAYE), seems to take no notice of this word. Perhaps he considered it as redundant: "signifying allegorically by that which is drunk the faith and promise," &c.—Account of the Writings and Opinions of Clement of Alexandria, London, 1835, 8vo, p. 386. It is not improbable that ἐναργὲς may be intended to denote the life and vigour of true faith.

* Ὁ Λόγος τὰ πάντα τῷ νηπίῳ, καὶ πατὴρ καὶ μητὴρ, καὶ παιδαγωγὸς καὶ τροφεύς· φάγεσθέ μου, φησὶ, τὴν σάρκα, καὶ πίεσθέ μου τὸ αἷμα. Ταύτας ἡμῖν οἰκείας τροφὰς ὁ Κύριος χορηγεῖ, καὶ σάρκα ὀρέγει καὶ αἷμα ἐκχέει καὶ οὐδὲν εἰς αὔξησιν τοῖς παιδίοις ἐνδεῖ· ὢ τοῦ παραδόξου μυστηρίου! Ἀποδύσασθαι ἡμῖν τὴν παλαιὰν καὶ σαρκικὴν ἐγκελεύεται φθορὰν, ὥσπερ καὶ τὴν παλαιὰν τροφήν· καινῆς δέ ἄλλης τῆς Χριστοῦ διαίτης μεταλαμβάνοντας, ἐκεῖνον, εἰ δυνατὸν, ἀναλαμβάνοντας, ἐν ἑαυτοῖς ἀποτίθεσθαι, καὶ τὸν

this passage the author had in view a spiritual eating and drinking, and not merely, if at all, a sacramental one. And this must be still farther evident to any who will take the trouble candidly to examine the whole context.

The writings of this father contain other passages, expressing the union of the true Christian with Christ, under the figure of drinking his blood. The reader will look in vain for any very lucid exposition of our Lord's discourse, although he will most probably acquiesce in the correctness of Bishop Kaye's remark, that while "Clement gives various interpretations of Christ's expressions in the 6th chapter of St. John's Gospel respecting his flesh and blood, in no one instance does he interpret them literally" (p. 447). In the language of the pious, very learned, but mystical and allegorizing father himself, " the Word is often employed in an allegorical sense, and so also is meat, and flesh, and food, and bread, and blood, and milk. ALL (IS) THE LORD TO BE ENJOYED BY US WHO BELIEVE ON HIM."* This one remark shows conclusively that, although he may have occasionally expressed his views in an obscure and confused manner, his thoughts and affections rose above the significative symbols to the blessed person who was thereby signified.

σωτῆρα ἐνστερνίσασθαι · ἵνα καταρτίσωμεν τῆς σαρκὸς ἡμῶν τὰ πάθη.—Ubi sup., p. 102.

* Πολλακῶς ἀλληγορεῖται ὁ Λόγος, καὶ βρῶμα, καὶ σὰρξ, καὶ τροφὴ, καὶ ἄρτος, καὶ αἷμα, καὶ γάλα· ἅπαντα ὁ Κύριος, εἰς ἀπόλαυσιν ἡμῶν τῶν εἰς αὐτὸν πεπιστευκότων.—P. 105.

That ORIGEN did not understand this language of our Lord's discourse at Capernaum in its literal sense, is undeniable from his own declaration. "There is in the New Testament a letter which kills him who does not understand spiritually what is said. For if you follow what is said, 'Except ye eat my flesh and drink my blood,' according to the letter, this letter killeth."* Accordingly, he gives various expositions of the phraseology, but always figurative, and states expressly that " we are said to drink the blood of Christ, not only in the rite of the sacraments, but also when we receive his words, in which life consists, as he himself says, 'The words which I have spoken are spirit and life.' He, therefore, was wounded [for our sins†], whose blood we drink, that is, receive the words of his doctrine."‡

In applying the directions in Exod., xii., 8, *seq.*, respecting the passover, to what is said of Christ in John, xix., 32–36, i., 29, and vii., 52, *seq.*, among other remarks, he says : " This is observed by me because John, in his Gospel, says, ' And the bread

---

* Est in Novo Testamento litera, quæ occidat eum qui non spiritaliter quæ dicuntur adverterit. Si secundum literam sequaris hoc ipsum quod dictum est, nisi manducaveritis carnem meam, et biberitis sanguinem meum, occidit hæc litera.—In Levit. Hom., vii., Opera, edit. Bened., Paris, 1738, tom. ii., p. 225.

† He had just before quoted Isa., liii.

‡ Bibere dicimur sanguinem Christi, non solum sacramentorum ritu, sed et cum sermones ejus recipimus, in quibus vita consistit, sicut et ipse dicit, verba quæ locutus sum, spiritus et vita est. Est ergo ipse vulneratus, cujus nos sanguinem bibimus, id est, doctrinæ ejus verba suscipimus.—In Num. Hom., xvi., tom. ii., p. 334.

which I will give is my flesh for the life of the world.' But now we eat the flesh of the lamb and the unleavened bread with bitter herbs, when by repenting of our sins we are afflicted with that godly sorrow which worketh in us a repentance to salvation not to be repented of."*

" If 1 suffer persecution and confess my Christ before men, I am certain that he also will confess me before his Father who is in heaven. If famine come, it cannot disturb me; for I have the bread of life which comes down from heaven and refreshes hungry souls. Neither can that bread ever fail, for it is perfect and eternal." †

" They shall not be confounded in the evil season, &c. By the evil season is meant the time of judgment. And in the days of dearth they shall have enough. He calls the days of dearth those in which many of the unclean are deprived of the bread of him who said, I am the bread that came down from heaven."‡

---

* Τοῦτο δέ μοι τετήρηται διὰ τὸ καὶ ἐν τῷ κατὰ Ἰωάννην λέγεσθαι· καὶ ὁ ἄρτος δέ ὃν ἐγὼ δώσω, ἡ σάρξ μοῦ ἐστίν ὑπὲρ τῆς τοῦ κόσμου ζωῆς· ἤτοι δὲ διὰ τὰς ἐπὶ τοῖς ἁμαρτήμασιν ἡμῶν μετανοίας τὴν κατὰ θεὸν λύπην λυπουμένων, μετάνοιαν εἰς σωτηρίαν ἀμεταμέλητον ἡμῖν ἐργαζομενήν, ἐπί πικρίδων ἐσθίομεν κρέα τοῦ ἀμνοῦ, καὶ τὰ ἄζυμα.—Comment. in Johan., tom. x. ; Opera, tom. iv., p. 177.

† Persecutionem si patiar et confitear Christum meum coram hominibus, certus sum quia et ille me confitebitur coram patre suo qui in cœlis est. Fames si affuerit, turbare me non potest ; habeo enim panem vitæ qui de cœlo descendit et reficit animas esurientes. Nec aliquando potest panis iste deficere, est enim perfectus et æternus. —Comment. in Epist. ad Rom., lib. vii., tom. iv., p. 607.

‡ Οὐ καταισχυνθήσονται ἐν καιρῷ πονηρῷ, καὶ τ. ε.) Καιρὸν πονηρὸν λέγει τὸν τῆς κρίσεως χρόνον, καὶ ἐν ἡμέραις λιμοῦ χορ-

"Man did eat angels' bread, &c.] The Saviour says, 'I am the bread that came down from heaven.' This bread, therefore, was formerly eaten by angels, but is now by men. To eat, in this place, signifies to know. For the mind eats what it knows, and what it doth not know it doth not eat."*

" If we speak those things that are perfect, that are robust, that are of the stronger sort, we set before you the flesh of the Word of God to be eaten."†

On Matthew, xxvi., 19, Origen applies language in this chapter to the Lord's Supper. Speaking of a spiritual understanding of the law, he says, that " by a spiritual celebration we fully perform all that is therein commanded to be done bodily. For we put away the old leaven of malice and wickedness, and celebrate the passover in the unleavened bread of sincerity and truth; Christ feasting along with us, according to the will of the Lamb, who saith, 'Except ye shall eat my

τασθήσονται. Ἡμέρας λιμοῦ ὀνομάζει ἐν ἇις πολλοὶ τῶν ἀκαθάρτων στερίσκονται τοῦ ἄρτου τοῦ εἰπόντος· ἐγώ εἰμι ὁ ἄρτος ὁ ἀπὸ τοῦ οὐρανοῦ καταβάς.—Selecta in Psal. (xxxvi., 19), Opera, tom. ii., p. 654.

* Ἄρτον ἀγγέλων ἔφαγεν ἄνθρωπος, καὶ τ. ε.] Ὁ Σωτὴρ φησιν· ἐγώ εἰμι ὁ ἄρτος ὁ ἐκ τοῦ οὐρανοῦ καταβὰς. Τοῦτον ὄυν τὸν ἄρτον ἤσθιον μὲν πρότερον ἄγγελοι, νυνὶ δὲ καὶ ἄνθρωποι. Τὸ ἐσθίειν ἐνταῦθα τὸ γινώσκειν σημαίνει: τοῦτο γὰρ ἐσθίει νοῦς ὃ δὲ γινώσκει, καὶ τοῦτο οὐκ ἐσθίει ὃ ὂυ γινώσκει.—Ibid., p. 771. Compare, also, on Isaiah, Hom. iii., Opera, tom. iii., p. 111.

† "Si perfecta loquimur, si robusta, si fortiora, carnes vobis Verbi Dei apponimus comedendas."—In Num., Hom. xxiii., Opera, tom ii., p. 359.

flesh and drink my blood, ye shall not have life in you.' "*

The next writer to be adduced is AUGUSTIN, the celebrated Bishop of Hippo.

"They said to him, 'What shall we do that we may work the work of God?' For he had said to them, 'Work for the food that doth not perish, but endureth to eternal life.' 'What shall we do?' say they; 'by observing what shall we be able fully to perform this precept?' Jesus answered and said to them, ' This is the work of God, that ye believe on him whom he hath sent.' This, therefore, is to eat the meat that doth not perish, but endureth to eternal life. Why do you prepare the teeth and stomach? Believe, and you have eaten.—No one fulfils the law but he who is aided by grace, that is, the bread which comes down from heaven. Love is the fulfilling of the law, the compendium

* "Spiritaliter celebrantes implemus omnia quæ illic corporaliter celebranda mandantur. Expellimus enim vetus fermentum malitiæ et nequitiæ, et in azymis sinceritatis et veritatis celebramus pascha, Christo nobiscum coepulante secundum voluntatem agni dicentis, nisi manducaveritis carnem meam, et biberitis sanguinem meum, non habebitis vitam manentem in vobis."—In Matt. Comment., tom. iii., p. 896. Compare, also, p. 899, and see p. 837, where the same application is made. The passage from Origen, above given, is quoted by AQUINAS in his Catena on St. Matthew. But the reader will bear in mind that, both in the original Latin of the "Angelical Doctor," and also in the translation, published at Oxford in 1842, of the "Aurea Catena" (recommended for family use!), the clause, "Christ feasting along with us," is omitted. It is, however, highly important, as it bears upon Origen's view of the meaning of John, vi., 54, and shows it to be figurative and spiritual.—See Divi THOMÆ AQUINATIS, Doct. Angel., Ordin. Prædic., Opera, Venet., 1775, 4to, tom. v., p. 380. English translation, p. 837.

of it, as the apostle says, 'Love, not of money, but of God; love, not of earth, not of heaven, but of him who made heaven and earth.' Whence is this love to man? Let us hear him: The love of God, says he, is poured forth into our hearts by the Holy Spirit whom he hath given us. The Lord being about to give the Holy Spirit, called himself the bread that came down from heaven, exhorting us to believe in him. For to believe in him, this is to eat the living bread. He who believes eats, is invisibly nourished (literally, fattened), because he is invisibly born again."*

After saying, that from various causes many may die, notwithstanding the use of ordinary food, he remarks: "But it is not so in this meat and drink, that is, in the body and blood of the Lord. For he who does not take it (the food, *esca*, as he had before called it) has not life, and he who does take it has life, and, indeed, eternal. By this food and drink he will denote association with the body and his members, which is the holy Church in his

---

* As it is unnecessary to quote the whole of the original Latin, I shall limit myself to those parts which have a direct bearing on the subject. "Hoc est opus Dei, ut credatis in eum quem misit ille. Hoc est ergo manducare cibum non qui perit, sed qui permanet in vitam æternam. Utquid paras dentes et ventrem? Crede et manducasti."—In Johan. Evang., cap. 6, Tract. xxv., § 12, edit. Bened., tom. iii., pars ii., Ant. 1700, p. 354. "Nemo implet legem, nisi quem adjuverit gratia, id est panis qui de cœlo descendit. Daturus ergo Dominus Spiritum Sanctum, dixit se panem qui de cœlo descendit, hortans ut credamus in eum. Credere enim in eum, hoc est manducare panem vivum. Qui credit, manducat; invisibiliter saginatur, quia invisibiliter renascitur."—Ibid., Trac. xxvi., § i., p. 357, 358.

predestinated, and called, and justified, and glorified saints, and faithful ones.—The sacrament of this thing, that is, of the union with (or unity of) the body and blood of Christ, is prepared, in some places daily, in others after intervals of some days, at the Lord's table, and received from the Lord's table, by some to life, by others to destruction; but the thing itself of which it is the sacrament, to every man who partakes of it for life, to none for destruction."*

"Finally, he now explains how that may be done of which he speaks, and what it is to eat his body and drink his blood. He that eateth my flesh and drinketh my blood abideth in me and I in him. To abide in Christ, and to have him abiding in us, is, therefore, what is meant by eating that food and drinking that drink. And, consequently, he who does not abide in Christ, and in whom Christ does not abide, undoubtedly does not spiritually eat his flesh nor drink his blood, although carnally and visibly he press with his teeth the sacrament of Christ's body and blood; but

---

* ' In hoc vero cibo et potu, id est, corpore et sanguine Domini, non ita est. Nam et qui eam non sumit, non habet vitam; et qui eam sumit, habet vitam, et hanc utiqûe æternam. Hunc itaque cibum et potum societatem vult intelligi corporis et membrorum suorum, quod est sancta ecclesia in prædestinatis, et vocatis, et justificatis, et glorificatis sanctis, et fidelibus ejus.—Hujus rei sacramentum, id est, unitatis corporis et sanguinis Christi alicubi quotidie, alicubi certis intervallis dierum, in Dominica mensa præparatur, et de mensa Dominica sumitur, quibusdam ad vitam, quibusdam ad exitium; res vero ipsa cujus sacramentum est, omni homini ad vitam, nulli ad exitium quicumque ejus particeps fuerit."—Ibid, § 15, p. 302.

rather eats and drinks the sacrament of so great a thing to his condemnation."*

On verse 63: "They thought he was about to distribute his own body, but he said that he was about to ascend into heaven, and, indeed, entire. When you shall see the Son of Man ascend where he was before, then certainly you will see that he does not distribute his own body in the way you think; then certainly you will understand that his grace is not consumed by bites."†

He concludes by urging as the all-important point, "that we be careful not to receive (literally *eat*) the flesh of Christ and the blood of Christ only in the sacrament, which many even bad men do; but to eat and drink so as to partake of the Spirit, so as to abide in the Lord's body as members, so as to grow strong by his Spirit."‡

---

* "Denique jam exponit quomodo id fiat quod loquitur, et quid sit manducare corpus ejus, et sanguinem bibere. Qui manducat, etc. Hoc est ergo manducare illam escam et illum bibere potum, in Christo manere et illum manentem in se habere. Ac per hoc qui non manet in Christo et in quo non manet Christus, proculdubio nec manducat [spiritaliter] carnem ejus, nec bibit ejus sanguinem [licet carnaliter et visibiliter premat dentibus sacramentum corporis et sanguinis Christi]; sed majis tantæ rei sacramentum ad judicium sibi manducat et bibit."—Ibid., § 18, p. 362. The words enclosed in brackets are in the printed editions, but are not contained in any of the manuscripts used by the Benedictine editor.

† "Illi putabant eum erogaturum corpus suum, ille autem dixit se adscensurum in cœlum, utique integrum. Cum videritis filium hominis adscendentem ubi erat prius, certe vel tunc videbitis quia non eo modo quo putatis erogat corpus suum; certe vel tunc intelligetis quia gratia ejus non consumitur morsibus."—Ibid., xxvii., § 3.

‡ "Hoc ergo totum ad hoc nobis valeat, delectissimi, ut carnem Christi et sanguinem Christi non edamus tantum in sacramento, ouod et multi mali; sed usque ad Spiritus participationem manduce-

In his treatise on Christian Doctrine, the same father comments on the 53d verse thus: "Unless ye eat, &c. He seems to order a crime or wickedness. It is, therefore, a figure, enjoining on us to communicate in the Lord's passion, and sweetly and usefully to lay up in memory that his flesh was crucified and wounded for us."*

These passages prove that Augustin did not regard the eucharist as directly and primarily intended by our Lord in this discourse; but doubtless he considered the eating and drinking therein urged as most effectually performed by the believer through that sacrament. Hence he sometimes employs the language of the discourse as he would have done if he had understood it to refer directly to the eucharist, and passages to this effect have been adduced in support of the charge of inconsistency, while, perhaps, they merely show a want of accuracy and fulness in the exposition of his views. One of the most remarkable occurs in his treatise on the desert and remission of sins and the baptism of infants, in which he endeavours to prove the necessity of giving the eucharist even to them. "Let us hear the Lord, I say, speaking not of the sacrament of the

---

mus et bibamus, ut in Domini corpore tanquam membra maneamus, ut ejus Spiritu vegetemur."—Ibid., § 11.

* "Facinus vel flagitium videtur jubere: figura est ergo, præcipiens passioni Dominicæ communicandum, et suaviter atque utiliter recondendum in memoriâ, quod pro nobis caro ejus crucifixa et vulnerata sit."—De Doct. Christ., lib. iii., cap. xvi., § 24, Opera, tom. iii., pars i., p. 40.

laver, but of that of his holy table, unless ye eat my flesh and drink my blood, ye shall have no life in you." And after quoting Titus, iii., 5, in reference to baptism, and John, vi., 51, 53, as directly referable to the eucharist, he infers the necessity of both these sacraments to the salvation of infants as well as adults. "Neither salvation nor life eternal is to be expected for any one without baptism and the body and blood of the Lord; in vain, without these, is it promised to infants."*

The controversial character of this work may account, in part, for such an extravagant position, although it affords no sufficient apology for it. In his sermons, also, on St. John's Gospel, he applies language taken from the sixth chapter to the eucharist, while, at the same time, it is evident that he considers the spiritual eating and drinking as what is chiefly intended, the eucharist being only the sacrament of this. Whether he meant to instruct his hearers that the discourse was *directly intended* of the Lord's Supper, or that indirectly it *includes* it as a principal means of grace, or is *only applicable* to it, admits of doubt. I leave the settlement of this point to those who are well versed in the voluminous writings of Augustin,

* "Dominum audiamus, inquam, non quidem hoc de sacramento lavacri dicentem, sed de sacramento sanctæ mensæ suæ: nisi manducaveritis carnem meam, et biberitis sanguinem meum non habebitis vitam in vobis.—Nec salus nec vita æterna sine baptismo et corpore et sanguine Domini cuiquam speranda est, frustra sine his promittitur parvulis." Da pec. merit. et remiss., lib. i., cap. xx. xxiv., § 26, 34, Opera, tom. x., p. 10, 13.

and of the fathers in general. If I may venture to express an opinion founded on but imperfect knowledge, I should be inclined to believe that the good bishop is not very accurate in explaining his views; and that, in common with the fathers of the second, third, and fourth centuries, he often applies certain Scriptural expressions to some one definite point, while he would by no means have maintained that such point was intended by the original writer or speaker. This last remark has a bearing on the whole subject of quotations, not excepting several of those which are found in the New Testament.

" As we have heard in the reading of the Gospel, the Lord Jesus Christ exhorted to eat his flesh and to drink his blood, with the promise of eternal life. Not all of you who heard this have nevertheless understood its meaning. Ye who are baptized and faithful know what he meant."* This is certainly intended of the eucharist, the mysteries which were concealed from catechumens and ordinary hearers. He then proceeds to urge the exhortation of St. Paul in 1 Cor., xi., 29, and to apply the language of John, vi., 56, 57. In his previous sermon, he remarks that the body and blood of Christ are life to every one, but imme-

* " Sicut audivimus, cum sanctum Evangelium legeretur, Dominus Jesus Christus exhortatus est promissione vitæ æternæ ad manducandam carnem suam et bibendum sanguinem suum. Qui audistis hæc, nondum omnes intellexistis. Qui enim baptizati et fideles estis, quid dixerit nostis."—Sermo cxxxii., de verbis Evang. Johan. 6, Opera, tom. v., p. 449, 450.

diately adds the qualification, "if what is visibly taken in the sacrament is also spiritually eaten and drunk in very truth."* This he illustrates by quoting the 63d and 64th verses.

JEROME, in his epistle to Hedibia, explaining Matt., xxvi., 29, does call "the Lord's body" (in the eucharist) "the bread that came down from heaven." But it must be evident to every reader that the whole tenor of the place is figurative. He does not hesitate to say, that "the patriarch Jacob desired to eat this bread when he said, 'If the Lord God will be with me, and give me bread to eat and raiment to put on.' For as many of us as are baptized into Christ have put on Christ, and eat angels' bread, and hear the Lord proclaiming, 'My meat is to do the will of the Father who sent me, and to finish his work.' Let us, therefore, do the will of him that sent us, the Father, and finish his work, and Christ will drink his own blood with us in the kingdom of the Church."†

On Isaiah, lxvi., 17 : "Tropologically we may

---

* "Tunc autem hoc erit, id est, vita unicuique erit corpus et sanguis Christi, si quod in sacramento visibiliter sumitur in ipsa veritate spiritaliter manducetur, spiritaliter bibatur."—Ibid., Sermo. cxxxi., p. 447.

† "Hunc panem et Jacob patriarcha comedere cupiebat, dicens, si fuerit Dominus, &c. Quotquot enim in Christo baptizamur, Christum induimus, et panem comedimus angelorum, et audimus Dominum prædicantem, meus cibus est, etc. Faciamus igitur voluntatem ejus qui misit nos Patris, et impleamus opus ejus ; et Christus nobiscum bibet in regno ecclesiæ sanguinem suum."—Ad Hedib., Opera, edit. Bened., Paris, 1706, tom. iv., pars i., p. 172.

give the meaning thus: All lovers of pleasure rather than of God are sanctified in gardens and in thresholds, because the mysteries of truth cannot enter, and they eat the food of impiety while they are not holy in body and soul; neither do they eat the flesh of Jesus nor drink his blood, of which he says, 'He that eateth my flesh and drinketh my blood hath eternal life.' For Christ, our passover, is sacrificed; who is eaten not without, but in one house and within:"* meaning, I presume, in the Church and in the heart.

"We read the Holy Scriptures. I suppose the Gospel to be the body of Jesus, the Holy Scriptures his doctrine. And when he says, he that doth not eat my flesh and drink my blood, although it may also be understood in the mystery, yet the word of the Scriptures, the divine doctrine, is more truly the body of Christ and his blood. If, when we go to the mystery—he that is faithful understands—if one falls into sin, he is in peril. If, when we hear the word of God, and the word of God and the flesh of Christ and his blood is poured into our ears, and we are thinking of something else, how great danger do we incur!"†

---

* "Secundum tropologiam possumus dicere, omnes voluptatis majis amatores quam amatores Dei sanctificari in hortis et in liminibus, quia mysteria veritatis non valent introire, et comedere cibos impietatis, dum non sunt sancti corpore et spiritu; nec comedunt carnem Jesu, neque bibunt sanguinem ejus. De quo ipse loquitur, qui comedit carnem meam, et bibit sanguinem meum, habet vitam æternam. Etenim pascha nostrum immolatus est Christus. Qui non foris, sed in domo una et intus comeditur."—Comment. in Isa. Proph., lib. xviii., tom. iii., p. 506.

† "Legimus sanctas scripturas. Ego corpus Jesu Evangelium

I conclude this representation by a quotation from one of the epistles of Basil: "Whosoevei eateth me, he says, liveth by me. For we eat his flesh and drink his blood, being made partakers, through his incarnation and natural life, of the Word and of wisdom. For his whole mystical sojourn in the flesh he calls flesh and blood, and his doctrine, consisting of practical, and natural, and theological, he manifested, by which the soul is nourished."*

From these quotations, and from many others which the writings of the fathers afford, it is evident that the minds of these holy men dwelt upon a spiritual union with Christ, in which their great

puto; sanctas scripturas puto doctrinam ejus. Et quando dicit, qui non comederit carnem meam et biberit sanguinem meum, licet in mysterio possit intelligi, tamen verius corpus Christi et sanguis ejus sermo scripturarum est, doctrina divina est. Si quando imus ad mysterium—qui fidelis est intelligit—si in maculam ceciderit, periclitatur. Si quando audimus sermonem Dei, et sermo Dei et caro Christi et sanguis ejus in auribus nostris funditur, et nos aliud cogitamus, in quantum periculum incurrimus!"—Breviarium in Psalt., cxlvii., 3, Opera, tom. ii., Appendix, p. 504.

* " Ὁ τρώγων μέ, φησι, ζήσεται δι' ἐμέ · τρώγομεν γὰρ ἀυτοῦ τὴν σάρκα, καὶ πίνομεν ἀυτοῦ τὸ ἁιμα, κοινωνοὶ γινόμενοι διὰ τῆς ἐνανθρωπήσεως, καὶ τῆς ἀισθητῆς ζωῆς τοῦ λόγου καὶ τῆς σοφίας · σάρκα γὰρ καὶ ἁιμα πᾶσαν ἀυτοῦ τὴν μυστικὴν ἐπιδημίαν ὀνόμασε · καὶ τὴν ἐκ πρακτικῆς καὶ φυσικῆς καὶ θεολογικῆς συνεστῶσαν διδασκαλίαν ἐδήλωσε, δι' ἧς τρέφεται ψυχή."—Epis. 141, Opera, edit. Paris, 1618, tom. ii., p. 928. I have translated ἀισθητῆς by *natural*. Its literal meaning is *perceived by the senses*.

Other citations from the fathers may be found in the works already mentioned, and also in L'Arroque's History of the Eucharist, part ii., chap. iv. This curious and valuable work was originally written in French, a translation of which, in one quarto volume, was published in London in 1684.

happiness consisted, and that they understood our Lord's language to be intended of this. It is also evident that they considered this union as effected and maintained, in a great degree, through the instrumentality of the sacraments which Christ had instituted, and therefore applied language expressive of the spiritual union to those means of advancing it, without particularly and critically defining the meaning and appropriating the application of every phrase. They were rather intent on the thing itself, than fastidious in choosing the terms whereby to express it.—See *Appendix*.

I shall conclude this Essay by referring to a few of the most prominent divines, in order to show that the general views already presented coincide with those of our best standard writers.

I omit the comments of CALVIN, LUTHER, and MELANCTHON, illustrious names in the Church, characterized respectively by far-reaching thought, by boldness in defence of truth, and by a meekness of wisdom and extent of learning seldom equalled. It is unnecessary to adduce their testimony in detail. It may be considered as comprehended in the language of the very learned and laborious GERHARD: "What is said in John, vi., 53, does not relate to the sacramental, but spiritual eating and drinking of the body and blood of Christ, which is necessary for the salvation of all."* The language of ERASMUS, however,

* "Dictum Joh., vi., 53, non de sacramentali sed spirituali corporis et sanguinis Christi manducatione et bibitione tractat, quæ om

is most especially worthy of the reader's attention, as he cannot be supposed to be a prejudiced witness, and few will venture to accuse him of incompetency. His notes on this chapter are, indeed, meager and very brief. Perhaps he did not choose to express himself fully. But he does expressly say, on verse 51, "if any one eat of this bread he shall live forever, that the ancients interpret this passage of heavenly doctrine."* CAMERON, a very learned and able commentator, observes, on verse 53, that the language here and elsewhere employed denotes "the power and efficacy of faith, by which we are united to Christ."† JAMES CAPEL says of the same verse: "These words plainly show that it was the duty of Christ's hearers at that time to have eaten his flesh, and therefore that this discourse is not to be restricted to a manducation in the eucharist or by the mouth, but that the body of Christ is to be eaten spiritually; and this is abundantly confirmed by the whole series of the discourse."‡

The same view is given by the most distinguished divines of the English Church. The com-

nibus ad salutem necessaria est."—De Sacra Cæna, cap. xxi., § 230, p. 190. Loc. Theol., tom. v. Franc. et Hamb., 1657.

* "Hunc locum veteres interpretantur de doctrina cœlesti."—Crit. Sac. on John, tom. vi., p. 115, edit. Amst., 1698.

† "His locutionibus significatur fidei vis et efficacia qua unimur Christo."—Ibid., p. 125.

‡ "Hæc verba perspicue docent jam tum debuisse Christi carnem ab auditoribus manducari, eoque non esse restringendam hanc orationem ad manducationem eucharisticam oralemve, sed spiritualiter esse manducandum Christi corpus: quod et tota series orationis abunde confirmat."—Ibid., p. 130.

mentary of WHITBY is accessible to all, and his exposition is so well known as to make any citations superfluous. His learned predecessor, Dr. HAMMOND, paraphrases the 47th and 48th verses thus: "He that embraceth my doctrine, and is sincerely my disciple, to believe and practice what I command him, shall undoubtedly live forever, as having fed on that enlivening bread, verse 33, receiving me his spiritual food by his faith into his soul." On the 50th and 51st he remarks: "The bread which is now sent you down from heaven will give immortality to them that feed on it, that is, to all that truly believe in Christ, that receive his doctrine, and digest it into the food and nourishment of their souls.—Whosoever feedeth, that is, believeth on me, embraceth my doctrine, and practiseth accordingly, shall not die; the soul whose food I am shall become immortal in bliss." So, also, on verse 53: "Except you thus feed on this celestial food, that is, be sincere disciples of the crucified Saviour;" and on verse 56: "He that thus feedeth or believeth on me, that resigns himself up to be ruled by me, is so made a member of me, that, by the life which is in me, he shall also be enlivened by God, by whom I live." On verse 63: "It is not the gross carnal eating of his body of flesh that he could speak of, but certainly a more spiritual divine eating or feeding on him; his words (see verse 68), that is, his doctrine, being spiritually fed on by them, that is, being received into their hearts," &c. On the next verse, for the words, "there are some of you that believe not," he substitutes, "for this spiritual feeding, sinking down this spiritual food into your hearts, there are some of you that are far enough from doing so." He expresses himself, also, to the same effect in his note, speaking of the "food which endureth to everlasting life," as "that doctrine of his which is food for their souls, and that grace which should be purchased by his death;" of "faith, here expressed by feeding on this spiritual food, not only eating, but digesting and turning it into the nourishment of our souls." He does not even allude to the eucharist, and evidently does not consider the discourse as originally intended of it, although undoubtedly he never meant to deny that the spiritual feeding on Christ by faith in that holy ordinance is comprehended within the terms of the general command.

In the same way, BISHOP BEVERIDGE represents the general sense of our Lord's expressions in this chapter. After quoting several verses, and closing with the 63d, he proceeds thus: "Whereby he plainly discovered that all that he had said concerning eating his flesh and drinking his blood is to be understood only in a spiritual sense. Not that we could eat that very flesh which he assumed, and drink that very blood which was spilt upon the cross; that is so absurd and impossible, that no man in his senses can take his words in such a carnal sense as that. But his meaning is, that he, having taken our flesh upon him, and offered it up, together with the blood thereof, as a sacrifice for the sins of the world, they who believe in him do as really partake of that sacrifice, and of all the benefits of it, as if they had eaten of the very flesh that was sacrificed, as the Jews did of the paschal lamb. By which means, Almighty God, being atoned and reconciled to them, gives them that Holy Spirit which is united to, and always accompanieth, the flesh of Christ, to be a standing principle of new life in them, to nourish and strengthen them with all true grace and virtue, as truly and really as our bodies are fed and supported by what we eat and drink. So that the whole drift and design of this divine discourse is briefly comprehended in that short sentence wherewith he begins it, and which may serve as a key to open all that follows, saying, 'Verily, verily, I say unto you, he that believeth on me hath everlasting life,'" verse 47.* He then goes on to remark, that the eating and drinking in the Lord's Supper is to be understood in the same sense, being spiritual and done by faith.

I have before directed the reader's attention to Dr. WATERLAND, who defends the same view of our Lord's discourse in his masterly work on the eucharist already referred to. These great divines of the Church of England were distinguished even among the learned for their extensive acquaintance with the fathers, for whose opinions,

* Sermon on the Preference of Spiritual Food to Natural. Sermons, vol. v., p. 312, 313, London, 1709

too, they entertained very high respect. And yet, with a thorough knowledge of all that antiquity contains on the subject of John, vi., they do not hesitate to express themselves as above stated. Let, then, the tyro in theology, who, by the help of the Latin column, or, it may be, of some modern English translation, has succeeded in mastering a few sentences of some Greek father, hesitate, with becoming modesty, before he decides against the learned judgment of these brightest luminaries of their age.

The following extracts from the writings of the most remarkable man of the English reformation may form a suitable conclusion. The opinions of ARCHBISHOP CRANMER were formed after much study and careful comparison of the Scriptures and fathers. Few divines of any age are comparable to this great man for acquaintance with patristical and scholastic theology, and his representations of the views of the early writers of the Church merit very particular attention. I trust no apology is necessary for the copiousness of the following extracts. I give them in the order in which they occur in his printed works.

Purposing to "set forth the very words that Christ himself spake both of the eating and drinking of his body and blood, and also of the eating and drinking of the sacrament of the same," he quotes John, vi., of the former, and remarks thus: "As touching this meat and drink of the body and blood of Christ, it is true, both he that eateth and drinketh them hath everlasting life, and also he that eateth and drinketh them not hath not everlasting life. For to eat that meat and drink that drink, is to dwell in Christ and to have Christ dwelling in him.* And therefore no man can say or think† that he eateth the body of Christ or drinketh his blood, except he dwelleth in Christ and hath Christ dwelling in him. Thus have ye heard of the eating and drinking of the very flesh and blood of our Saviour Christ."

He then proceeds to the latter point. "Now as touching the sacraments of the same, our Saviour Christ did institute them in bread and wine at his last supper which he had with his apostles the night before his death."‡

"Christ in that place in John spake not of the material and sacramental bread, nor of the sacramental eating (for that was spoken two or three years before the sacrament was first ordained§), but he spake of spiritual bread, many times repeating, I am the bread of life which came from heaven, and of spiritual eating by faith, after which sort he was at the same present time eaten of as

---

* Augustin in Joan., Tract. 26.

† Aug., de Civitate, lib. 21, cap. 25.

‡ The Remains of THOMAS CRANMER, D.D., Archbishop of Canterbury, collected and arranged by the Rev. HENRY JENKYNS, M.A., in four volumes. Oxford, vol. ii., p. 292, 293. A Defence of the true and Catholic Doctrine of the Sacrament of the Body and Blood of our Saviour Christ, book i., chap. ii., iii.

§ This is a mistake, as the discourse was delivered at Capernaum about a year before the institution of the eucharist, namely, near the passover preceding the last. See John, vi., 4.

many as believed on him, although the sacrament was not at that time made and instituted. And therefore he said, ' Your fathers did eat manna in the desert, and died ; but he that eateth this bread shall live forever.' Therefore, this place of St. John can in no wise be understood of the sacramental bread, which neither came from heaven, neither giveth life to all that eat it. Nor of such bread could Christ have then presently said, this is my flesh ; except they will say that Christ did then consecrate so many years before the institution of his Holy Supper."*

" Wherefore, to all them that by any reasonable means will be satisfied, these things before rehearsed are sufficient to prove that the eating of Christ's flesh and drinking of his blood is not to be understood simply and plainly as the words do properly signify, that we do eat and drink him with our mouths ; but it is a figurative speech, spiritually to be understood, that we must deeply print, and fruitfully believe in our hearts, that his flesh was crucified and his blood shed for our redemption. And this our belief in him is to eat his flesh and to drink his blood, although they be not present here with us, but be ascended into heaven. As our forefathers, before Christ's time, did likewise eat his flesh and drink his blood, which was so far from them, that he was not yet then born."†

* Ibid., book ii., chap. x., p. 338, 339.
† Ibid., book iii., chap. x., p. 381, 382.

In arguing against Dr. Smith, who alleged the 6th chapter of St. John in defence of transubstantiation, he says: "I answer by his own reason. Can this promise be verified of sacramental bread? was that given upon the cross for the life of the world? I marvel here not a little of Mr. Smith's either dulness or maliciousness, that cannot, or will not, see that Christ, in this chapter of St. John, spake not of sacramental bread, but of heavenly bread; nor of his flesh only, but also of his blood and of his godhead, calling them heavenly bread that giveth everlasting life. So that he spake of himself wholly, saying, 'I am the bread of life: he that cometh to me shall not hunger, and he that believeth in me shall not thirst forever.' And neither spake he of common bread, nor yet of sacramental bread; for neither of them was given upon the cross for the life of the world.

"And there can be nothing more manifest than that, in this sixth chapter of John, Christ spake not of the sacrament of his flesh, but of his very flesh. And that, as well for that the sacrament was not then instituted, as also that Christ said not in the future tense, 'The bread which I will give shall be my flesh,' but in the present tense, the bread which I will give is my flesh; which sacramental bread was neither then his flesh, nor was then instituted for a sacrament, nor was after given to death for the life of the world.

"But as Christ, when he said unto the woman of Samaria, 'The water which I will give shall spring into everlasting life,' he meant neither of material water nor of the accidents of water, but of the Holy Ghost, which is the heavenly fountain that springeth unto eternal life; so, likewise, when he said, 'The bread which I will give is my flesh, which I will give for the life of the world,' he meant neither of the material bread, neither of the accidents of bread, but of his own flesh; which, although of itself it availeth nothing, yet being in unity of person joined unto his divinity, it is the same heavenly bread that he gave to death upon the cross for the life of the world."*

" The same flesh was also given to be spiritually eaten, and was eaten, indeed, before his supper, yea, and before his incarnation also. Of which eating, and not of sacramental eating, he spake in the sixth of John: 'My flesh is very meat, and my blood is very drink: he that eateth my flesh and drinketh my blood dwelleth in me and I in him.'"†

" But your understanding of the sixth chapter of John is such as never was uttered of any man before your time, and as declareth you to be utterly ignorant of God's mysteries. For who ever said or taught before this time, that the sacrament was the cause why Christ said, if we eat not the flesh of the Son of Man, we have no life in us? The spiritual eating of his flesh and drinking of his blood by faith, by digesting his death in our minds

---

* Vol. ii. The Answer of Thomas, Archbishop of Canterbury, &c., against the false Calumniations of Dr. Richard Smyth, p. 9, 10.

† Ibid., p. 64. Answer to Gardyner, book 1.

as our only price, ransom, and redemption from eternal damnation, is the cause wherefore Christ said, that if we eat not his flesh and drink not his blood, we have not life in us; and if we eat his flesh and drink his blood, we have everlasting life. And if Christ had never ordained the sacrament, yet should we have eaten his flesh and drunken his blood, and have had thereby everlasting life, as all the faithful did before the sacrament was ordained, and do daily when they receive not the sacrament. And so did the holy men that wandered in the wilderness, and in all their lifetime very seldom received the sacrament, and many holy martyrs, either exiled or kept in prison, did daily feed of the food of Christ's body, and drank daily the blood that sprang out of his side (or else they could not have had everlasting life, as Christ himself said in the Gospel of St. John), and yet they were not suffered, with other Christian people, to have the use of the sacrament.

"And that, in the sixth of John, Christ spake neither of corporeal nor sacramental eating of his flesh, the time manifestly showeth. For Christ spake of the same present time that was then, saying, 'The bread which I will give is my flesh: and he that eateth my flesh and drinketh my blood, dwelleth in me and I in him, and hath everlasting life.' At which time the sacramental bread was not yet Christ's flesh, for the sacrament was not then yet ordained; and yet, at that time, all that believed in Christ did eat his flesh and drink his blood, or else they could not have dwelled in Christ, nor Christ in them.

"Moreover, you say yourself, that in the sixth of St. John's Gospel, when Christ said, the bread is my flesh, by the word 'flesh' he meant his whole humanity, as is meant in this sentence, the Word was made flesh; which he meant not of the word 'body,' when he said of bread, this is my body, whereby he meant not his whole humanity, but his flesh only, and neither his blood nor his soul. And in the sixth of John, Christ made not bread his flesh when he said, the bread is my flesh; but he expounded in those words what bread it was that he meant of, when he promised them bread that should give them eternal life. He declared in those words, that himself was the bread that should give life, because they should not have their phantasies of any bread made of corn. And so the eating of that heavenly bread could not be understood of the sacrament, nor of corporeal eating with the mouth, but of spiritual eating by faith, as all the old authors do most clearly expound and declare."*

"When Christ said, 'The bread which I will give is my flesh, which I will give for the life of the world,' if he had fulfilled this promise at his supper, as you say he did, then what needed he after to die that we might live, if he fulfilled his promise of life at the supper."†

"Faithful Christian people, such as be Christ's

* Ibid, p. 65–67.   † Page 81

true disciples, continually from time to time record in their minds the beneficial death of our Saviour Christ, chawing it by faith in the cud of their spirit, and digesting it in their hearts, feeding and comforting themselves with that heavenly meat, although they daily receive not the sacrament thereof, and so they eat Christ's body spiritually, although not the sacrament thereof. But when such men, for their more comfort and confirmation of eternal life, given unto them by Christ's death, come unto the Lord's holy Table, then, as before they fed spiritually upon Christ, so now they feed corporally also upon the sacramental bread. By which sacramental feeding in Christ's promises their former spiritual feeding is increased, and they grow and wax continually more strong in Christ, until at the last they shall come to the full measure and perfection in Christ. —We say, that as they eat and drink Christ in the sacrament, so do they eat, drink, and feed upon him continually, so long as they be members of his body."*

"This I say, that the fathers and prophets did eat Christ's body and drink his blood in promise of redemption to be wrought. Although, before the crucifying of his flesh and effusion of his blood, our redemption was not actually wrought by Christ, yet was he spiritually and sacramentally present, and spiritually and sacramentally eaten and drunken, not only of the Apostles at his last

* Ibid., book iii., p. 130, 131.

Supper, before he suffered his passion, but also of the holy patriarchs and fathers, before his incarnation, as well as he now is of us after his ascension."*

" As concerning these words of Christ, the words which I do speak be spirit and life, I have not wrested them with mine own gloss, as you misreport, but I have cited for me the interpretation of the Catholic doctors and holy fathers of the Church."†

May the author and reader of this treatise practically understand what the father of the English Reformation meant by spiritually eating and drinking the body and blood of Christ, and may each know, by his own blessed experience, what it is to dwell in Christ and to have Christ dwelling in him! Amen!

* Ibid., p. 139. † Page 187.

APPENDIX.

In the third part of the preceding essay, the reader will find a pretty full view of the commentary of the fathers of the first four centuries on those verses of our Lord's Discourse, which are thought by some writers to have been intended principally of the eucharist. These venerable authors have so often been referred to as containing the direct sacramental interpretation of the discourse, that I must be allowed to request the reader's very particular attention to that part of the essay. And, in order to develop still further the exposition of certain of the most distinguished personages of by-gone ages, I have thought it might be useful to imbody some of their teachings in an Appendix.

That the sacramental interpretation of the discourse in John sixth should become prominent was, of course, to be expected, just in proportion as the religious condition of the Church tended to the external and ceremonial, in contradistinction to the inward and the spiritual. And such was really the fact. Yet even in those periods of comparative ignorance, which we have probably been too apt to turn away from with disgust as the Dark Ages, unworthy of notice, in which nothing is expected to be found that will repay the trouble of search, glimpses of the pure ray may be seen, proving that the "holy light" was far from being quenched, and that the same blessed Spirit who beamed upon the soul of the beloved disciple still "shone inward," and taught "the hearts of his faithful people." Let any one read the commentary of the venerable Bede, of the eighth century, on our Lord's Discourse at Capernaum, and while he will recognize the sacramental interpretation, he can not fail to perceive, also, that the leading current of the author's thought flows strongly toward the spiritual. "*Moses gave you not the bread from heaven, but my Father gave you the bread from heaven:* That manna, therefore, was significant of the imperishable meat, and all those were signs of me. My signs ye loved; what was signified thereby ye despise. *And the bread which I will give is my flesh:* Whosoever will live, let him believe in Christ; let him eat spiritually the spiritual food, and become incorporated with the body of Christ; and let him not be a corrupt member, meriting excision, but let him be fair and sound, fit for his Head." Afterward he proceeds in the words of St. Augustin, as quoted in the Essay, p. 128, 129.* In another place he explains the verse last referred to, both of the eucharist and of the atonement made on the cross: "This bread the Lord then gave when he delivered the mystery of his body and blood to the disciples, and when he offered himself to God the Father on the altar of the cross."†

The sacramental view is prominent in the exposition of the Bulgarian metropolitan of the eleventh century, THEOPHYLACT, although he does not entirely lose sight of the spiritual and deeper sense. "*The bread which I will give*, &c.: Here he evidently speaks of the mystical reception of his body. But, indicating his right—for not as a slave (servant), and inferior to his Father, was he crucified, but willingly—he says, 'I will give my flesh for the life of the world.' For although it is said that he was given by the Father, yet also that he gave himself. But consider that the bread which is eaten by us in the mysteries is not

---

* *Non Moyses dedit vobis panem de cælo, sed pater meus dedit vobis panem de cælo. Operamini cibum qui non perit*, &c. Ergo et illud manna hoc significabat, et illa omnia signa mea erant. Signa mea dilexistis; quod significabatur, contemnitis.—*Et panis quem ego dabo caro mea est pro mundi vita:* Quisquis vivere vult, credat in Christum, manducet spiritualiter spiritualem cibum. Incorporetur corpori Christi, et non sit putridum membrum, quod resecari mereatur, sit pulchrum, sit sanum, sit aptum capiti suo.—Venerabilis BEDÆ Presbyteri in Sanctum Evangelium B. Joannis Expositio, cap. vi. Opera; Colon., 1688, tom. v., col. 509, 510.

Hunc panem tunc Dominus dedit, quando mysterium corporis et sanguinis sui discipulis tradidit, et quando semetipsum Deo Patri obtulit in ara crucis.—D. THOMÆ AQUINATIS Doct. Angel. Ord. Præd. Opera; Venet., 1775, 4to, tom. iv., p. 429: Super Joannis Evang. Catena, cap. vi.

a type of the Lord's flesh, but the flesh itself; for he did not say, the bread which I will give is a type of my flesh—but is my flesh. For, through the mystical blessing and the addition of the Holy Spirit, it is transformed by inexplicable (literally, ineffable) words to the flesh of the Lord. And now, therefore, the bread is changed into the Lord's flesh." But still he does not forget the necessity of an inward character correspondent with the holiness of the sacramental elements. "When, therefore, we hear the words, 'Except ye eat the flesh of the Son, ye have no life,' it becomes us, in receiving the divine mysteries, to have unwavering faith, and not to inquire into the manner: for the animal man, that is, he who is led by human and carnal or natural reasonings, doth not receive what is supernatural and spiritual, and therefore has no conception of what the spiritual food of the Lord's flesh means."*

Let us look now at the language of the celebrated Abbot of Clairvaulx in the twelfth century. St. Bernard speaks of " a three-fold reception of the body and blood of the Lord. The first is both sacramental and spiritual, of which the Lord says, *He that eateth my flesh and drinketh my blood dwelleth in me and I in him*. And again: *He that eateth me shall live on account of me*. The second, which is only spiritual, as the Lord himself says again, *The flesh profiteth nothing, it is the spirit that*

* Φανερῶς δὲ ἐνταῦθα περὶ τῆς μυστικῆς μεταλήψεως τοῦ σώματος αὐτοῦ, φησιν· ὁ ἄρτος γάρ, φησιν, ὃν ἐγὼ δώσω, ἡ σάρξ μου ἐστὶν, ἣν ἐγὼ δώσω ὑπὲρ τῆς τοῦ κόσμου ζωῆς· τὴν ἐξουσίαν δὲ αὐτοῦ δεικνύων, ὅτι οὐχ ὡς δοῦλος, καὶ ἐλλάττων τοῦ πατρὸς αὐτοῦ ἐσταυρώθη, ἀλλ' ἑκὼν, φησιν, ὅτι ἐγὼ δώσω τὴν σάρκα μου ὑπὲρ τῆς τοῦ κόσμου ζωῆς· εἰ γὰρ καὶ δεδόσθαι λέγεται ὑπὸ τοῦ πατρὸς, ἀλλὰ καὶ ἑαυτὸν δεδωκέναι.—Πρόσχες δὲ, ὅτι ὁ ἄρτος ὁ ἐν τοῖς μυστηρίοις ὑφ' ἡμῶν ἐσθιόμενος, οὐκ ἀντίτυπόν ἐστι τῆς τοῦ Κυρίου σαρκὸς, ἀλλ' αὐτὴ ἡ τοῦ Κυρίου σάρξ. Οὐ γὰρ εἶπεν, ὅτι ὁ ἄρτος ὃν ἐγὼ δώσω ἀντίτυπόν ἐστι τῆς σαρκός μου, ἀλλ' ἡ σάρξ μου ἐστί. Μεταποιεῖται γὰρ ἀπορρήτοις λόγοις ὁ ἄρτος οὗτος διὰ τῆς μυστικῆς εὐλογίας, καὶ ἐπιφοιτήσεως τοῦ ἁγίου πνεύματος, εἰς σάρκα τοῦ Κυρίου..... Δεῖ τοίνυν ἡμᾶς ἀκούσαντας, ὅτι ἐὰν μὴ φάγωμεν τὴν σάρκα τοῦ υἱοῦ, οὐκ ἔχομεν ζωὴν, ἐν ταῖς μεταλήψεσι τῶν θείων μυστηρίων πίστιν ἔχειν ἀδίστακτον, καὶ μὴ ζητεῖν τὸ, πῶς ; ὁ γὰρ ψυχικὸς ἄνθρωπος, τουτέστιν, ὁ λογισμοῖς ἀνθρωπίνοις καὶ ψυχικοῖς ἤτοι φυσικοῖς ἑπόμενος, οὐ δέχεται τὰ ὑπὲρ φύσιν καὶ πνευματικά. Ὥσπερ οὖν καὶ τὴν πνευματικὴν βρῶσιν τῆς τοῦ Κυρίου σαρκὸς οὐ νοεῖ, κ. τ. λ.—Commentarius in Joannem, cap. vi. Opera ; Venet., 1754, tom. i., p. 593–595.

quickeneth. As if he had said, If ye understand a carnal reception only without grace, it is of no use, but rather injurious: but the spiritual without the carnal quickeneth thee. Of the third, which is only sacramental, the apostle speaks when he says, *He that eateth and drinketh unworthily, eateth and drinketh judgment to himself, not discerning the Lord's body;* that is to say, not distinguishing it from other food."*

The remarks of the celebrated Cardinal Hugo de Sancto Caro are equally worthy of note. This very distinguished man belongs to the former half of the thirteenth century. He died in 1260.† I quote from his Postilla on St. John's Gospel, printed at Basle, in connection with his other works, in five folio volumes.—Verse 50. " *That if any one eat of it:* by believing and loving; or by receiving worthily his flesh and blood." 51. " *If any one eat of this bread:* either, if any one worthily receive the eucharist; or, (if) any one by faith and love unite Christ to himself, and convert his words and example into his own nourishment. *He shall live forever:* provided he persevere therein." 53. " *Except ye eat:* by faith, as says Augustin: Believe, and thou hast eaten." See p. 126 of the Essay. Afterward he proceeds to note " three things in the sacrament of the eucharist: the species of bread, the true body of Christ, and Christ's mystical body. The first is only the sign; the second, the sign and the thing signified; the third is only the thing signified. The first is taken only sacramentally; the second sacramentally and spiritually; the third only spiritually. The first

---

* De prima sumptione, quæ est sacramentalis et spiritualis, Dominus dicit: *Qui manducat meam carnem et bibit sanguinem meum, in me manet et ego in eo:* et rursum, *Qui manducat me, vivet propter me.* (It is worthy of remark that the abbot has given the exact meaning of the original διὰ with an accusative, *propter*.) De secunda, quæ est tantum spiritualis, iterum ipse Dominus loquitur: *Caro nihil prodest, spiritus est qui vivificat;* ac si diceret: si intelligis tantum carnalem sumptionem absque gratia, nihil prodest, immo nocet; spiritualis vero absque carnali te vivificat. De tertia quæ est tantum sacramentalis, dicit Apostolus: *Qui manducat et bibit indigne, judicium sibi manducat et bibit, non dijudicans corpus Domini:* quod est dicere, non discernens corpus Domini ab aliis cibis.—Instructio Sacerdotis de tribus præcipuis mysteriis, cap. xii. Opera; Paris, 1719, vol. ii., col. 548. † Cave, Hist Lit., vol. ii., p. 300; Oxon., 1743.

and second may be taken by both good and bad in common; the bad man to his death, the good to his life. But only the good man can receive the last; for, to eat the mystical body of Christ is nothing else than, by faith, hope, and love, to become incorporated in the unity of the Church." To the same purpose, afterward, "*Except ye eat:* spiritually or by faith; or, taking the antecedent for the consequent, except you are united by love to the Son of God, who is the Son of man."* His comment contains much more to the same purpose, proving conclusively that, although he does not lose sight of the eucharist, he never fails to represent the eating and drinking as a spiritual reception of Christ through virtue of an inward union with him by faith; and this as the main point of instruction in this portion of the Discourse.

After the reader has carefully considered the views of the fathers both of the early and Middle Ages, as they have now been presented to him, he will be the less surprised at the action taken on John sixth by the celebrated Council of Trent. The learned divines of this synod well knew that they could not maintain the sacramental interpretation on the ground of the consent of the fathers. In the course of the discussions which arose on the subject of giving the cup to the laity, this chapter was appealed to in order to show that our Lord speaks indifferently of eating his flesh and drinking his blood, and also simply

---

* *Ut si quis ex ipso manducaverit:* credendo et amando; vel digne carnem ejus et sanguinem sumendo.—*Si quis manducaverit ex hoc pane:* seu, si quis eucharistiam digne sumpserit, vel quis Christum fide et amore sibi junxerit, et verba ejus et exempla in nutrimentum suum converterit. *Vivet in eternum:* Si in hoc perseveraverit.—*Nisi manducaveritis:* per fidem, secundum illud Augustini, Crede et manducasti.—Nota tria esse in sacramento eucharistiæ; speciem panis, corpus Christi verum, corpus Christi mysticum. Primum est signum tantum; secundum signum et res; tertium res tantum. Primum sumitur tantum sacramentaliter; secundum sacramentaliter et spirituallier; tertium tantum spiritualiter. Primum et secundum potest sumere communiter bonus et malus; sed malus ad mortem, bonus ad vitam. Tertium non potest sumere nisi bonus. Nam corpus Christi mysticum manducare nihil aliud est quam fide, spe et charitate unitati ecclesiasticæ incorporari.—*Nisi manducaveritis:* spiritualiter, seu per fidem. Vel ut sumatur antecedens pro consequenti, nisi uniti fueritis per charitatem filio Dei. qui est filius hominis.

of eating his flesh; and hence it was inferred that the latter virtually comprehends the former. But, in opposition to this, it was urged that "many fathers understood those places in St. John not of sacramental, but of a spiritual eating of Christ's flesh and drinking of his blood; and therefore that the council should not indirectly sanction the opposite interpretation."* Cardinal Seripando, who presided on that occasion, remarked that there were two controversies connected with the discourse in that chapter of St. John; one with the heretics, on this point, whether the communion in both kinds was therein divinely commanded and made necessary for the salvation of all the faithful; and the other among the Catholics themselves, whether the discourse related to sacramental or spiritual communion: that, even allowing St. John to speak of the former, the inference that the cup was absolutely necessary to salvation was erroneous; and that the proposed decree decided nothing in reference to the second of the two controversies. The "modest" cardinal, as Pallavicini calls him, should have stated the point somewhat differently; for the controversy was not whether the cup is absolutely necessary to salvation, but whether the command to drink it is not as plain and obligatory as that to eat the flesh, and therefore the drinking of the one as certainly necessary to salvation as the eating of the other. After much consideration and discussion, it was agreed that, in reference to our Lord's Discourse, the decree should be amended by adding the words, "However, among the various interpretations of the holy fathers and doctors, it may have been understood."† This passed by a majority of twenty-six, eighty-three voting in favor of the amendment, and fifty-seven against it. The minority did not maintain that the chapter related directly to the eucharist. They took the ground "that it was not in character with the

* Che in quel testo de S. Giovanni intendevasi da molti Padri non il mangiamento e il bevimento sacramentale, mà lo spirituale della carne e del sangue di Christo; et che non conveniva al Concilio statuir obliquamente la contraria interpretazione.—Istoria del Concilio di Trento, scritta dal Padre Sforza Pallavicino; Rom., 1657, cap. xi., lib. xvii., p. 403.

† Comunque frà le varie interpretazioni de' Santi Padri e de' Dottori s'intenda.—P. 409

dignity of the council to say any thing about the uncertainty of the meaning of so celebrated a portion of Scripture, and by express terms to leave it doubtful; and that it would be more decorous to adhere to the original form of the decree, and not to mention the second controversy at all."*

That such were the views and action of the Council of Trent is candidly admitted by Dr. Wiseman.† Mr. Johnson, too, has certainly the best reason for saying, "It is evident that the Council of Trent did not believe the discourse in the sixth chapter of St. John to speak strictly of sacramental eating and drinking."‡ But he is undoubtedly mistaken in giving what follows as an "especial" cause why they did not limit the meaning of the discourse to the sacramental exposition: "Because it was apprehended that if John sixth were taken as meant of the eucharist, it must follow that it was absolutely necessary that the people must communicate in both kinds." The language of Cardinal Seripando, already quoted, expressly disclaims such an apprehension, inasmuch as it denies the inference to be well founded. It is indeed true, as the author remarks, that "our Saviour declares it to be altogether as dangerous to omit the drinking of his blood as the eating of his flesh;" and the correctness of the conclusion he draws as to the necessity of the cup would be undeniable if the eucharist were the direct subject of the chapter. But that the divines of this council would have allowed this conclusion is quite another matter. The inference drawn from the indifferent use of the phrases *eating the flesh and drinking the blood*, and from the former alone, namely, that this comprehends the other, shows that they would not; and it is plain that the presiding cardinal expressly denies it. The result is irresistible, that the leading theologians of the Church of Rome at that period knew well that they could not claim a consent of fathers for the sacramental interpretation of John sixth.

* Allegavano questi, non esser dignità del Concilio, recando un capo sì celebre della Scrittura, toccar la dubieta del senso, e insieme lasciarla con aperte parole in sospeso: maggior decoro serbarsi nella prima forma, in cui non si menzionava la controversia.—P. 409.
† Lectures on the Real Presence; Lect. v., p. 163–165.
‡ The Unbloody Sacrifice; London, 1718, p. 154.

A calm and candid attention to these particulars in the history of the interpretation of this chapter, and also in that of the Council of Trent, can not fail to be instructive. If men will but divest themselves of prejudice, and take the necessary trouble in order to secure the truth, they must see that the exposition of John sixth which has most generally prevailed in all periods of the Church is that of spiritual feeding on Christ by faith, and that, to use the language of Hooker, either "in the sacrament" or "*otherwise;*"[*] the former means having been always regarded as the most important. Loose assertions, which have no better support than an assumed meaning of certain figurative words in this chapter, can therefore have no influence on those who are conscientiously bent on seeking, finding, and keeping the truth of God's most holy word.

[*] Book v., sect. 55; Oxford, 1793, vol. ii., p. 219. Compare the language in section 60, p. 248: "By sacraments and *other* sensible tokens of grace."